I0120245

Arthur Dillon

River Songs

And Other Poems

Arthur Dillon

River Songs
And Other Poems

ISBN/EAN: 9783744713351

Printed in Europe, USA, Canada, Australia, Japan

Cover: Foto ©Thomas Meinert / pixelio.de

More available books at **www.hansebooks.com**

RIVER SONGS

AND OTHER POEMS,

BY

ARTHUR DILLON

Author of " Gods and Men."

ILLUSTRATED BY

MARGERY MAY

NEW EDITION.

REMINGTON & CO., LTD., LONDON AND SYDNEY,
1893.

All Rights Reserved.

POEMS.

ILLUSTRATIONS.

RIVER SONGS.

I HAVE heard the ceaseless gurgle of the hurrying water-brook
As it purled beneath the briars hiding in covert nook,
And I've walked adown his windings and tracked his snaky
    way
To where the gentle river came out into the day ;
And the going of the waters tended ever towards the sea,
But I stayed by the gentle river till it should speak to me.
One song for all hath the ocean, thus hath the Poet sung,
But every river, beck, and brook speaks with its own, own
    tongue ;
Yea each new drop of water singeth another song,
And each knows not whence nor whither the other goeth
    along,
And each telleth each his story as they hurry on their way,
And their telling is the murmur that they murmur by night and
    day.
Ah ! but let me disentangle from the endless skein of song
This story which one water-drop sang as he flowed along.

B

And this is the song that he sang me, as I stood among the
    reeds ;
Where the trees were thinly scattered and the woodland met
    the meads.

Lo ! Spring had strewn the coppice with carpeting of flowers,
And the streamlet flowed among them, brimful with recent
    showers,
And joyous sang the streamlet to the flowers as he passed,
And they waved their heads and nodded : 'The winter hath his
    blast.'
Cried the flowers to the streamlet : ' But now is time to play,'
And the streamlet gave a merry laugh and hurried on his way.
But I was in the streamlet, a-nestling in his hair,
And I paused behind a greeny stone where the moss grew soft
    and fair,
Which checked a part and let a part go by it at a bound,
Where a last year's oakleaf like a ship sailed ever round and
    round ;
And I spoke to the shrivelled oakleaf if I might learn its lore,
But the life had left its fibres, and it could speak no more.
But upon the bank above me stood dancing in the air,
A throng of wood anemones, starry and passing fair :
White as the mist of mountains, yet with a flush of morn,
They seemed the work of fairies or jewels a fay had worn.
And thus sang all their voices : ' Why ask you of the dead ?
Ask rather lore of the living.'   And I turned to them and said :

'Most fair among the fairest of all that see this wood,
What story can ye tell me of things or bad or good?'
'Now speak not thus unto us, albeit you hold us fair,
For a fairer treads the forest and breathes this woodland air.'
Thus spake, in sooth, the flowers ; but answering them I said :
'I have been in the shady ocean, I have lain in the torrent's bed,
I have seen the stately icebergs and watched the setting sun ;
Of palaces of princes have I seen many a one ;
Yet never saw I such beauty.   Yet tell now unto me
What manner of fruit or flower, or stately fern or tree,
Is this surpassing loveliness that your bright eyes have seen?'
And they said : 'It is neither flower, nor tree bedight in green,
Nor fruit, nor fern, nor foliage ; but of the race of men :
As beautiful as sunrise, as pale and pure as when
The fleece-edged clouds are driven before the silver moon,
And their thin skirts are steeped in light more fair than light of
    noon.
She walketh here by the margin from death to birth of day,
And listens to the nightingale as he gives to the woods his lay ;
And she sometimes singeth beneath her breath a song of burn-
    ing love,
Soft as the coo of wood-pigeon in the antlered trees above.'
And I asked the starry flowers, flushed with the ruby stain :
'Whom loves this lovely lady?   And is she loved again?'
And they said : 'Her love is given to one far, far away,
Who has fared before on his journey to the land where mortals
    may.

But the earth lies on his bosom and the flowers nod on his
    breast,

For down beneath this very spot doth her murdered lover
    rest.'

'Now tell me,' I said, 'this story,' for they drooped their heads
    and sighed,

'In truth as sad a story as ever mote betide.'

'We saw it not,' said the flowers, 'but the wood hath kept
    the tale,

And yon holly bush in the winter hath kept it withouten fail.'

'Ah ! that I have,' said the holly—he spoke in a hollow tone—

'And since the deed, at Christmas my berries are never shewn,

But I pine like a tree that dieth, with thinking on the deed :

To think that he who loved so well by caitiff hand should
    bleed.

But she pineth not for her lover, for she knows him passing
    true ;

She deems him gone on a journey, voyaging the wide world
    through.

Still now and again in her walking a cloud comes o'er her
    brow,

When she shrinks to think of the ocean, lest it hold him even
    now.

But the trust is strong within her, strong as the doom of fate,

That in this wood they shall meet again if she shall only wait.'

But thus I asked the holly : 'When her lover left her last,

What words were his to the lady that her faith hath stood so fast ? '

' 'Twas more by each look and gesture than by any word he
 spoke,

Yet these his words,' said the holly; 'They stood beneath this
 oak.

"Shall I tell thee what I'm thinking when I'm past the realm
 of thought ?

When the high, cold arch of reason Love has shewn to be but
 naught.

Shall I tell thee of a chasm that could swallow up the sea?

Shall I tell thee of a passion that is that huge gulf to me?

Ah! tell thee? Can I tell thee what passeth spoken word,

What passeth sweetest music that e'er was sung by bird?

Lo! many years must part us now. But yet I will return,

And on this very spot we meet." Oh saw you ever burn

Two full bright stars on a frosty night? I wis so looked her
 eyes,

And he gazed right full into them; and they were as angels'
 cries :

Saying, "I love and trust you."

        'Thus parted they; and he

Went off upon his journey to travel by land and sea.

Now eve by eve she came here; and morn by morn she went;

And walked by the spreading oak-tree, with its limbs so gnarled
 and bent.

And a year came up in the springtime, waxt strong, and to his
 grave

Went down ere a second springtime the world her flowers gave.

And another year and another went after him to their doom ;
And a fourth year stood in their footprints, in early summer's
     bloom.
When back again from his journey unto the trysting-tree
Rode he who had left his lady there to roam the restless sea.
And jewels he brought his loved one, from the store of a foreign
     mart :
A necklace rare and a bracelet ; and more—a loving heart.
In passing pointed toward me the quick ears of his steed,
But he dismounted by the stream, too wrapt in thought to heed.
The sun was high in the heavens, so the lady was not there,
But he stood and thought of the words once breathed within
     that hallowed air.
Behind my dark green mantle, thick as the veil of night,
Crouched three, in rusty morions and leathern sarks bedight.
And they watched till his back was toward them : each with his
     steel in hand,—
His bright steel bare and ready.
                              'Then the leader of the band
Cried : "Dig him a grave by the stream here ; and delve him a
     bed in the clay,
That man may know not our doing nor the deed we have
     wrought this day."
So they brought them spades from the thicket where they had
     left them hid,
And the soil was soft by the water, and they cut through the
     roots amid.

Thus they dug him a grave by the margent, in haste in the
  sodden mould,
And they filled in the clay of the copsewood on his clay that
  was hardly cold.
And they trod the clay above him, with the will of a desperate toil ;
And hid it with moss and oakleaves ; and stole away with the
  spoil.

'And the lady came in the evening : she saw not the ground
  was stirred ;
But she sang as she was wont to sing or listened to the bird
That in the night pours out his soul in ever lovely song.
And she walks o'er the grave of her loved one, whom she hath
  loved so long ;
And she hath walked by the margent from that day unto this,
And she waits for him who can never come to seal her earthly bliss.'

And the holly bush was silent : he had no more to say,
And I stepped out sadly from my stone, and hurried on my way.
But later on in my travels I came to that place again :
In the gloom of a dying winter, when neither mist nor rain,
But a chilly sleet was falling, and the sky was grey and dark,
And the holly bush was a withered stem, as a dead man stiff
  and stark ;
But there was another holly now bright with the berry's pride,
And I asked him : 'What of the lady ?' and thus he said and
  sighed :

'See the oaktree torn from his holding, and the roots wrenched
up from the ground.

A wind has swept through the coppice ; and in his hair it
found

A hold, and dragged him downward and hurled him on his
side.

But his roots were strong and spreading, and stretched out far
and wide ;

And they rent a ghastly fissure and showed a ghastlier sight,

And the lady came in the evening when the moon was full and
bright,

And the moon shone into the hollow, on what was laid below ;

And the lady met her lover where he left her long ago.

Thus they met and never parted.'

                                  And he mingled with the stream,

And I felt like one who just awakes out of a ghastly dream.

But now above the music there rose a louder strain,

Than the roundelays the waters most sing : so now again

I listened to the measure, and marked the words he told,

As he sang thus to the River of the Water's Day of old.

Now listen, brothers of water, for I tell you again the tale,

That ye know so well of your freedom and your great
bacchanal. ˉ

For the word went forth o'er the waters : 'Behold you once were
free,

Ere the land rose out of the ocean and parted sea from sea.

And lo ! once more ye are loosened ; for once and never
    more,

I have lifted the doors of your prison and broken your bounds
    and your shore.

For lo ! my people are evil, and their deeds rise up to me

Like the loathsome fogs uprising from a putrid inland sea.

Now, therefore, to scourge my people, I give you revel on
    earth ;

Come up and confound them together, in midst of their sins
    and mirth.'

And the flood-gates of Heaven were opened, and the wells
    were unsealed in the deep,

And lo ! we rose in our volume. And the rivers did no more
    keep

Their courses ; but filled the valleys, until the mountains
    rose

Islands amid our forces, clad in eternal snows.

And, 'mid the snow and the waters, the people struggled and
    cried,

And toiled still upward in trembling, climbing the mountain
    side,

And their wail rose over our armies; and vain was the warrior's
    might ;

But he cast his shield in the waters, and his spear, for the
    hopeless flight.

And higher we rose, exulting, and higher, till, one by one,

Over mountain by mountain did hurrying waters run.

Knee-deep they stood on the mountains, beast and woman
and man,

Old folk and little children, huddled, dismayed and wan.

And the rain poured down from the heavens, and the flood-
gates opened beneath,

And we rose like angry lions that roar and gnash their teeth.

But the whole was done in the darkness, for the rain was there
seen no light ;

And we drowned the tops of the mountains, each with his
living freight.

Then wild we rushed o'er the kingdoms that were erst so rich
and fat,

While Leviathan was swimming o'er the peaks of Ararat.

Then we thought in pride that our power mankind should
overthrow ;

But we saw the great Ark rolling, drifting with the water's flow.

Then we sinned for indignation ; and we beat against the Ark,

And we gnashed our teeth in anger, seething in the sightless
dark.

Then pausing we took counsel, saying : 'Decide it now :

Ever slaves, or with the war horse and the ox that draws the plough

Whelming the Ark beneath us, to stand as once we stood

The possessors of Creation, when God saw that we were good.'

Then we drew ourselves together, and we strove with gathered
might,

Heaving up a mountain billow that should whelm the Ark
outright ;

And the thunderbolt of water fell shuddering on its side.
Three times to burst its timbers our utter strength was tried,
But the congregated waters of the water-homes, who drowned
All the world besides, were baffled ; the Ark rode safe and
    sound.
Then our hearts grew faint within us, and we neither struck
    nor spoke,
For we saw the doom relentless, and we bowed beneath the
    yoke.
Then the Word went forth : 'O waters, disperse ye to your
    seas,
Your lakes, and fens, and rivers, in their manifold degrees.'
And we, all the waters, heard it ; and down we sank thereat
And left the Ark high-stranded on the top of Ararat.
So vainly had we striven, battling with the ways of Fate ;
But to do the work appointed is rightly to be great.
And we often in our wanderings sing the story of the time
When God gave us grace to revel once again through every
    clime.

So he finished all his singing of the Deluge.   And his song
Died amid the many voices as the river flowed along.
But the next drop sang of maidens singing 'mid the morning
    dew,
And they furrowed dark the silver as riverward they drew
Where lovely youths came sailing, gentle, with fearless glance,
Who leaped out to the maidens and joined in song and dance,

Crying : 'Winter's storms are over ; with the song-birds let us
    sing !
And welcome, like the flowers, the fair promise of the spring.
Let the warm sun and the breezes be as wine to glad our
    hearts :
Let us leap like crownèd Bacchants, joyful that the cold
    departs.
Out of winter comes the summer, with her forehead white and
    clear ;
Let us bring the sound of music for the birthday of the year.
Birth is the type of death, and death is the second birth,
Where the free soul leaps to Heaven from the trammels of the
    earth.
So revel we in gladness and keep our Eastertide.'
Thus they leaped and danced across the fields that lay so green
    and wide.

Why should we ask a story ; or more within a song
Than the voice of such wild gladness as these had who tripped
    along?
Though ye sought I could not give it. Yet this I know,
    indeed,
I was full glad to see them as they danced athrough the mead.

So he ceased, and I stood idly looking at the water's flow,
Pondering of both men and rivers, whence they come and
    whither go ;

For even as the youths and maidens, in the song he sang
    to me,
Each with some unwritten story, seemed the water-drops to be.
But as I stood by the river I caught another strain,
And another drop of water, as it hurried to the main,
Sang thus; and I walked on with it, for I wis it would not stay.

I was by the Isle of Ernot, where the waves for ever and aye
Dash on the rocks : and the seaweed is wavèd to and fro,
As the waves come on with a rushing, and with a rush they go.
And there is a sound in the hollows, and a tale that is told by
    the caves,
And they sing the song of the island for ever to the waves.
And this is the song that they sing them from ebb to flow of
    the tide :

Lo ! Mildred ruled in Ernot when that her father died,
And she ruled it well and justly ; for a year she reigned its
    queen,
And thrice twelve wooers wooed her from across the ocean
    green,
And each sang his song unto her, and struck his harp to his
    song,
And told her how love within him burned tenderly and strong.
But thus she answered their singing, and the love that they
    told therein :
' My heart is won by no man ; nor may there man it win.

For unto God have I given my spirit, and all my love,

And on earth I may have no treasure, but in Heaven that is
above.'

But they grew sad when they heard her, at the words that she
spake and said ;

And they spake not a word, but sat there as silent as the dead.

Then every third man rose up, and went each one to his ship,

And lowered his streaming pennon till it beat the sea with its
tip ;

And loosed the sail from its bondage, and gave it to the breeze,

And fared o'er the ocean homeward, and left the isle in the
seas.

But stayed there twice twelve wooers, whose flames burned
bright and keen,

And thus they answered her, saying : 'O Mildred, Beautiful,
Queen,

Now bid us only, thy servants, and we will work thee thy will ;

For what more joy than to serve thee?' Then silent they sat,
and still,

Awaiting what she should bid them ; and thus she, answering,
said :

' May Holy Mary requite you each with blessings on his head !

Now listen, ye who have sought me from beyond the briny sea;

As yesternight I was sleeping, a dream came over me,

And a form of an angel radiant, with wings that wrapt him
round,

Stood by my bed and called me, his head with glory crowned.

"Sail forth, sail forth, and seek thou, though the way be strange
 and long,
That blissful Home of the Blessed that thou hast sought in
 song.
But learn thou first of a pilot who knoweth the way full well;
For many who careless sail the deep drift to the shores of
 Hell."
Thus ceased to speak the angel.   But go ye, learn ye the way:
Explore the coasts of all unknown lands till ye find the Gates
 of Day.
Then bring me word of your journey, and row me over the
 main,
And through the gates of Paradise, and leave the world and
 pain.'
But they grew sad as they heard her, at the words that she
 spake and said;
And they spake not a word, but sat there as silent as the dead.
Then every other rose up, and went each one to his ship
And lowered his streaming pennon till it beat the sea with its
 tip;
And loosed the sail from its bondage and gave it to the breeze,
And fared o'er the ocean homeward, and left the isle in the
 seas.

But the last twelve went together, and chose a ship that was
 new;
Sound and stout in the timbers, well seasoned oak and true.

And then they sware together, by God and His Saints on high,

That they shall roam o'er the ocean, and seek till they find or die.

And the new ship lay on the rollers, nor had felt the sea's kiss
    cold,

For the shipwright's latest work on her was barely two days old.

Queen Mildred stood by the carven prow, and they stood six
    on a side,

And they watched the flow of the lapping waves till the time of
    the highest tide,

And Mildred called her by a name: a name which meaneth *I seek*,

And they thrust her out on the waters with the pride of her
    gilded beak.

Then running all through the surges they swung them over her
    sides,

And Mildred prayed the Saints for them to send them winds and
    tides

That should carry them on their journey through scorching
    sun and ice,

To where the Saints for ever rest 'mid the joys of Paradise.

Now they braced the yard and loosed the sail, and spread it to
    the breeze,

And fared straight out they knew not where ; and left the isle
    in the seas,

And swift they cut through the dimpled waves, and the foam
    flew over their prow :

For the freesh breeze pressed behind their sail, and they felt
    glad in their vow.

As day and night they kept sailing over the laughing sea,
Three always watched in the nighttime, each watch watched
    hours three.
But as the third sun left them they hailed an unknown shore,
Where the cliffs rose out of the ocean worn with the waves and
    hoar ;
But the line of the cliffs was broken and a valley was mid the
    hills ;
And a reed-fringed river wandered down, fed by a thousand
    rills ;
And on the hills there were vineyards, with promise of ruddy
    wine,
Where, trailed from lofty pole to pole, basked the luxuriant vine ;
And in the midst of the valley rose, like a fairy's home,
A palace built on lofty piers with many a snow-white dome.
Now toward the river steered they, and landed from the brink :
Hasting to reach the palace before the sun should sink.
They passed through the olive gardens and the vineyards well-
    kept worth,
Till, as they neared the palace, came there a sound of mirth :
And there were the tones of singing and music with the song,
And the living notes came floating out with a merry ring and
    strong ;
And now they came to the spotless steps where all was still and
    lone :
But the sound of revelry within poured out in an endless
    drone.

So on they passed o'er the pavement into a princely hall,
Lit by the glare of blazing links fixed on the polished wall.
And a feast was spread out on the board, and the wine flowed
    in the bowls,
And the slaves held jars of goodly wine to sate their masters'
    souls,
And round the banquet feasting sat lords and ladies fair,
All habited in costly stuffs wrought o'er with colours rare,
And gold and rich embroidery with all the art of earth ;
And they laughed and drank in an endless whirl of music, wine,
    and mirth.
Now as those mariners passed up, seeking some one to say
Wherefore this gorgeous revel after the end of day,
They came to one who was serving the wine from his painted
    jar,
And they spake and said : ' We are strangers sailed hither from
    afar.
Now tell us wherefore this feasting and the name of this wine-
    blest land.'
And he set on the floor his empty jar, and answered the stranger
    band :
'This Isle is the Home of Revel, and whoso drinks of this
    ` wine
Forgets his joys, forgets his woes, and henceforth doth not pine
But joins the guests who fill this hall ; and drinketh deep and
    long,
And lives until his time to die in revel, wine, and song.

But we are they who tilled the land or ever they brought the
vine,

And now we toil the stranger's slaves ; nor drink we of the
wine.

Too well we know its blessings are but a deadly snare ;

For it can sooth not after death : it kills but earthly care ;

But I must go and fill again ere that they call for more.'

With that he stooped and took his jar from off the polished
floor,

And went and mingled with the rest. Then one guest called a
slave

And a full goblet of the wine into his hand he gave ;

And bade him take it to the twelve and seat them at the
board.

And so he held the cup to them and said, 'Good sirs, my
lord

Offers you wine and bids you sit and join them at their feast ;

That now at last from grief and care your souls may be
released.'

But they, forewarned of its fair guile, took not the proffered
draught,

But turned back through the dusky night to seek their strong-
built craft,

And now they passed through the darkness, led by the Ocean's
sound,

And groped their way through the vineyards, over the broken
ground,

And leaped down into their vessel, and thrust out oars from her
    side,

And from the Home of Revel fled across the unresting tide.

But now the fresh breeze held his breath and the blazoned
    sail hung sad,

Like to a lovelorn maiden left by him who could make her glad.

So they furled the sail on the long yard-arm, and lowered it down
    the mast ;

And fore and aft they braced it round, and made all firm and
    fast.

Then they sit them down upon the thwarts, six on a side, to
    row ;

And they strike the oars into the sea, and merrily on they go.

And they pull till the sun reddens the east ; and no one stands
    at the helm,

For they know not whether north or south they shall steer to
    find this realm.

Not till the mighty sun hath sunk into the ocean's flood,

Faint with the wounds of fight, to drown in a pool of his own
    blood,

They ship the oars.   Then praying each the Mother-maid to
    keep

Them through the night, they lay them down and turn them to
    their sleep.

And all night long they were drifting, as they slept, with the
    tide's still flow,

With the hollow sky above them and the hollow sea below.

But when the blushing dawn comes forth, lovely with golden
    hair,

They shake them from their drowsy sleep, the morning meal
    they share.

Then strike the sharp blades of their oars into the billowy
    sea ;

And on she goes beneath their strokes, like a seabird wild and
    free.

The sun comes up and the sun goes down and the sun comes
    up again,

And still all round about them lies the circle of the main.

And now the sun again hath turned and standeth in the
    west,

And seems to hover longingly over his place of rest,

When they descry a cloud that hangs brooding over a land,

And they ask each other, 'Can this be it?' and they pull for
    the unknown strand.

And over the rippling waves they go into a silent bay,

Where on the beach the listless seals in friendly sunlight lay.

Then they ran their ship up on the sand that lay so smooth
    and white,

And the wild seals knew no fear of them, but lay still in the
    light.

And they stepped down and crossed the sand and sought the
    swelling plain,

Where all seemed wrapt in a warm soft haze that was neither
    mist nor rain.

And the whole place loomed like one long dream ; a land
   where breeze was none :

Still as the lotos-eater's isle, or the home of the setting sun.

And they wandered on o'er the swelling lawns, leaving the
   silver shore,

Till a broad, low-lying vale, that seemed to sleep for evermore,

They see ; and through the mist a lake, smooth and as still as
   glass ;

And the clouds were mirrored on his face, and they did not
   change nor pass,

But hung for ever motionless in the broad expanse of blue ;

And the sky gazed ever at the lake and the lake at the sky he
   knew.

And they who had sailed from Ernot, over the throbbing
   deep,

Passed on to go into this vale where all things seemed asleep.

Then on the greensward stretched they saw, steeped in a
   drowsy charm—

A sleep that yet was not a sleep—thoughtless of good or harm,

Fair maidens and tall youths ; they seemed half drowned in
   the soft haze,

Like statues prone upon the grass they lay through all their
   days,

And they gleamed as gleams the silver moon when the cloud-
   veils make her dim,

For the warm mist on their bosoms lay, and on each smooth,
   white limb.

Now as the ship's crew, awe-bound, gazed on them lying there,
One wandered by in tattered weeds, haggard with grief and
    care.
Of her they asked, 'What isle is this?' she said, 'The Home
    of Sleep ;
And these are they who have lain down and ceased to smile or
    weep.
For whosoever once has flung his limbs upon this sod,
Sleeps fearless till his life is passed, nor knows of fiend or
    god.'
'And *then*?' they asked. 'Ah me ! and then?' she echoed.
    'Wherefore then?
One *then* is there for all who sleep or wake of mortal men.
But I have wandered, trembling long upon the brink of sleep ;
Too long.' With that she laid her down. Like one who has
    drunk deep
Of that enchanted draught whose taste subdues the drinker's
    mind,
So lay she ; while the furrows which but now her brow had
    lined
Passed, as the shadow of a cloud slips from a distant plain,
And left her features beautiful, untouched by joy or pain.
And from her limbs the tattered rags rolled in a curl of mist ;
And there in a new youth she lay, by the warm hazes kissed.
But no one saw ; for those who sailed out o'er the unknown
    deep
Knew that their haven could not be in the soft Home of Sleep,

So when they heard her tale, ere she into her trance had
    passed,
As men who fly a deadly plague that follows on the blast
They sped across the silent lawns to where the good ship lay,
And bent the oars beneath their strokes till they were far away.
And on they rowed through the ocean, over the midnight seas,
And from the part toward which they drew sprang up a sullen
    breeze.
And steady it blew against them, yet stronger hour by hour,
And close upon the leaden sea the leaden clouds did lower.
A cold grey light came from the east, where the sun was wont
    to rise,
But farther was no sign of sun through all the threatening skies.
And stronger blew the sullen breeze, steadily over their beak,
Till the bare mast beneath its force began to groan and creak,
And the rigging trembled in its breath, that held the sailless
    mast,
While over head an endless cloud was ever driven past.
Thus through a noontide swart as dusk they go, till one
    descries
Five ship-lengths' off where from the seas a rocky isle doth
    rise.
The air is still, under its lea ; now into a creek they run,
Where scarce they tell the rock from cloud, so hidden is the
    sun.
But safe between two naked steeps they leave the ship at rest,
And climb the sides of rugged crags, and gain a cheerless crest,

Where mid the driving cloud they stand, but on its upper
    edge

Where the sun's rays level with the mist strike a bare, splintered
    ledge.

There a man lay nailed down on the rock, with his flesh all
    torn with stones,

While yet and anon the heavy mist gave back his hollow groans.

Drawn by the sound they saw him and came to where he
    lay.

One hand only was nailed not, and with that did he flay

And tear himself with splinters plucked from the mountain's
    face ;

And by his side there rusting lay what seemed an iron mace.

' Now rend no more your body ; for we will set you free,

For Christ's love,' cried the seamen, but straightway answered he,

' Let be, let be, I beseech ye ; nor drive me back again :

For here alone on this mountain I know of naught but pain.'

Then thus they asked him : ' Teach us what land we have
    reached this day ? '

' Naught but my pain I know ! ' he answered as he lay.

But then did they take counsel, and did as they agreed :

They drew the nails from their places; the nailèd man they
    freed.

But he released turned angry, and said : ' Ye have wrought me
    wrong.

For my care strikes back upon me with a sting more sharp and
    long

Than the nails ye have drawn from my body.' And they
asked him again : 'What land ?'

And he stood in their midst and pointed, stretching his wounded
hand.

Now there was a glow through the fog-veil, as from a furnace
door

That dyed the mists to crimson, that were else so cold and
hoar :

'Yonder,' said he, 'is the smithy, where men may forge them
their nails,

Or crooked hooks, that shall tear them, or sharp-toothed iron
flails.

Now hark, ye may hear the hammers, as they forge them their
means of pain.'

And they heard a sound as of metal struck, which echoed and
echoed again.

'And some there bathe in the furnace, and couch their limbs
on the coals ;

Till by the changeless doom of God they shall breathe out
their souls.

Thus themselves from their trouble, themselves from themselves
they hide,

Tortured or crushed they dying live, or scorched, or cruci-
fied.

So go ye down through the hollow and choose what ye hold the
worst,

But let me drive my nails again and live in pain and thirst.'

But turning round they left him, the restless seas to roam ;
But they heard him take the rusty mace and strike the irons
    home.
Clambering, they go from cleft to cleft, down to the narrow
    creek :
And from that dismal island they turned their gilded beak,
Hoisted a corner of the sail, and flying o'er the main,
Left those who sought a dreadful rest in the grim Home of
    Pain.

And now they wandered onward over the billowy sea,
Till all the air above them grew hushed as hushed may be,
And for nine days they were rowing where the sun seemed
    almost dead :
He rose far south like a wounded man who dying rears his head,
And lets it fall as he rears it, and breathes his soul away.
And on the tenth they were rowing at an hour that should be
    day ;
And all that day they were rowing but never a sun they saw,
And as they went into the north the air grew cold and raw.
And on they went through the darkness, where day was dark as
    night,
Day after day ; till from the north there shot a lovely light,
And they each one left his rowing and stood by the beakèd
    head,
And watched it rise in its beauty, and watched it circle and
    spread.

And each one said to other as he took again the oar,

''Tis it !' and they rowed with stouter hearts than they'd ever
rowed before.

And many days they were rowing over the silent sea,

While the sky was bright above them, as bright as bright may
be.

Then a whistling came behind them, like the wind among the
trees,

And they looked, and lo ! a flying troop came sweeping over
the seas,

And they heard their voices shouting and singing as they flew ;

And the sound of their wings and their voices, as they neared
them, louder grew.

' Welcome ! Welcome, O brothers ; for empty we do not come,

Rejoice with us now, O brothers ! Sing ye, and be not
dumb !

We were at the Home of Revel, where amid vines and bowers,

The folk grow fat for our pleasure and when they die are
ours ;

And we watched till the time of dying came down upon one
guest,

And our own to our own we are bringing, and we do but wait
for the rest ;

And a goodly herd were feasting, and sang in the palace hall,

Stout lords and dainty ladies, and we wait but to win them
all.'

And in the song they were past them, and the end came faint
    o'er the wave ;

Mixt with the wail of their captive whom they bore to the living
    grave.

And again the air was quiet, and they rowed on toward the
    light

That lit the pavement of the sea with a lovely glow and bright.

But again they heard behind a sound as of wings that beat the
    air,

And a sound as a wind that breaks the mast and the stout sail
    doth tear,

And a wingèd flock came sailing betwixt the sea and sky,

And they flung a song into the air and an exulting cry.

'Welcome to ye, O brothers, whom we have missed so long.

Rejoice ye, rejoice, O brothers ; and add your song to our
    song !

For we bring you tidings of gladness, that shall make you laugh
    and leap.

Lo ! as in the air we hovered over the Home of Sleep,

Where all who die are ours that rest in the twilight haze,

The doom came upon one who slept, and the end of his tale
    of days.

And our own to our own we are bringing.   And many are yet
    to come

Who sleep in the valley ; so sing ye, our brothers, and be not
    dumb ! '

And they flew on toward the brightness, and their song came
 faint on the breeze,

Like the lisping wind through the sedges or through the tops
 of the trees.

But the seamen rowed on toward the brightness, whither the
 troop had flown,

Though a doubt stole in upon them which they hardly dared
 to own,

If this bright light before them, though it shone so clear and
 fair,

Marked but the unmeasured Pit that shot through heaven a
 reddening glare.

And as they mused, from behind them came a rushing, as
 when a flood

Bursts from a banked-up river, and yellow with licked-up
 mud,

Pours itself in its fury headlong over the plain ;

And, behold, another flying crowd came scudding over the
 main ;

And the sound went hurtling before them, as they sang and
 shouted with glee :

And thus they sang, like trumpets, or the rush of the hoary
 sea :

' Welcome ! thrice welcome, O brothers ; but hear ye first
 what we bring,

Ere ye can rejoice as we rejoice, and sing as ye hear us sing,

By the Home of Pain we were watching, where whoso dies is
  ours ;
And as we watched a tortured one ended his tale of hours,
And our own to our own we are bringing.   But still there are
  more to bring,
For all day long at the forges we heard the hammers ring
As they forged them their pains ; and the hill-tops are rich in
  nailèd men.
We sing for ye, hearken, O brothers, and hear ere your eyes
  may ken.'

And they flew straight on before them, on toward the Northern
  Light ;
And they cast a shadow in their train, dark as the darkest night.
But the light beamed fair as ever, and the sea was smooth as
  glass ;
The sky was as a sapphire blue, as mote all thought surpass.
But now a lurid storm-cloud a-starboard hove in sight,
That seemed a fiend with beetling brow, strong in his evil
  might.
And a hoarse wind beat up the sea, and blew the foam like
  snow,
And nearer came the threatening cloud as wearily on they row
And the taut ropes quivered in the wind and the sky was over-
  cast,
But on they toiled through the foam and seas, till the turmoil
  should be past.

And on a sudden out they came, out of the mantling cloud ;
And to the west they saw the storm rush headlong, fierce and
    loud.
But now the northern glory shines brighter than earthly light,
Chaste and pure as the winter stars, and as the noon sun bright.
And lo ! they saw in the distance, towering sheer and tall,
Higher than highest home of kings, a bright and gleaming
    wall,
And there was a way up to the light cut through the walls of
    ice ;
And they spake no word but each one knew 'twas the steps of
    Paradise.
And as they gazed in wonder one of them spake and said :
' Let us turn no more but take our joy, in the Home of the
    Blessed Dead.'
But thus they answered him, saying : ' Now this we cannot do;
For Mildred, Queen of Ernot, sailed we the ocean through,
To seek her the way we have found here, and bring her word
    of the way,
Then sail again o er the ocean with her, to the shores of Day.'
Then answered he who had spoken : ' Go ; do ye as ye will.
Lo ! I will gain alone the land which knoweth naught of ill.'
With that he sprang out from the bows into the treacherous
    sea,
And struck out with a steady stroke ; but all in vain struck he :
Beneath a placid face the deep rushed with a current strong,
And though he struck out manfully it bore him swift along ;

Ever he headed towards the steps, and fought against the stream,

Till the dead waters numbed his limbs.   As in an evil dream

Whither we would not we are borne ; so in the ruthless tide

He swept to where a dismal cave opened its portals wide,

Far away to the misty west, and drank the deadly flood ;

Beneath the walls of ice it yawned with a look that froze the blood.

And they saw him washed into the cave by the cold stream of Death ;

While still they lay upon their oars, and hardly drew their breath.

But deep from the cavern's entrails they caught the words of a song

That on the air, o'er the water, came floating faint along :

'O joy, thrice joy thrice over.   Oh ! how can we tell in song

The joy we feel ? or give welcome to you who have toiled so long,

And have prowled, like wolves who gather round sheepfolds over the earth ;

And have brought us victims to sate us and gladden our hearts with mirth,

From the island homes of Revel, of Sleep, and of gloomy Pain :

Oh ! how can we give you greeting and welcome you back again ? '

Then many joined in a chorus that pealed out loud and strong,
Swelling like distant thunder, and these were the words of
    their song,
That, mixed with groans and stifled shrieks, came over the
    polished sea—
A song of joy and of triumph, and a song of exulting glee :

‘ Rejoice ! O rejoice together ! Make a glad noise and sing !
Oh be we joyous, O brothers, for this that time doth bring :
For those who sought in the Island of Revel, or Sleep, or
    Pain
From care a rest have passed to where they shall never rest
    again ! ’

But they who had sailed from Ernot sailed back across the
    deep,
And five men sat at a side to row, and one the helm did
    keep ;
And by the stars they taught them the course they should hold
    when they
Rowed out their beauteous Mildred to the bright shores of
    Day.
And on they rowed toward the sunlight out of the Polar Sea ;
Until again they saw the sun, and bright and strong was he.
And now they sailed with the breezes, and now they had to
    row,
But ever over the ocean merrily on they go.

At last they came to Ernot, where Mildred ruled as queen ;
And the ship moved in a wavy fringe of seaweed long and
green ;
And their cheeks were bronzed with the sunbeams, and their
brows were weatherworn,
For far and long on the ocean had they and their ship been
borne.

Now Mildred long had waited, and watched for their return,
And all night long in her tower she set a light to burn,
To guide them into the harbour ; and on either side the bay,
On the headlands, burning beacons ; and bade strict watch by
day
To mark their earliest coming ; and bring her word when a
sail
Hove over the long horizon.   And so withouten fail
They came to her and told her, and she hastened down to the
shore ;
And stood there waiting as their ship came steadily under the
oar.
And now the keel furrowed the beach and left the treacherous
main,
And as they landed she greeted them and welcomed them back
again.
And she led them up to the castle, and feasted them in hall,
And they told her all the wondrous things that did to them
befal'.

But many days they waste not ; but scrape their ship of the
weed :

And caulk her planks and repair her, according as there is need ;

Renewing her standing rigging, and seeing her shrouds be
strong.

Queen Mildred gave a sail she wrought while they were gone
so long,

Embroidered with gules and argent wrought in the sacred
sign

That blushed upon its dazzling breast, redder than reddest
wine.

Now at last they step into the ship and put her head to sea ;

Five men sit on a side to row, and the last by the helm stands
he.

And Mildred who reigned in Ernot, now leaves the land of her
sway,

To sail across the trackless deep, and seek the shores of Day.

And they set the sail on the long yardarm, and it takes the
freshening breeze,

And they sail away to come not back, and leave the isle in the
seas.

And on they sail to the northward by the way that they did
return ;

Until they leave the sun behind, and see the North light burn.

And the light beamed fair before them, and the sea was smooth
as glass :

And the sky was as a sapphire blue, as mote all thought surpass.

But now a lurid storm-cloud a-starboard hove in sight,
That seemed a fiend with beetling brow, strong in his evil
   might.
And nearer came the threatening cloud, but steadily on they
   go ;
Right over head it flies amain, swift as the wind can blow,
But down beneath the sea is calm, and a soft breeze swells the
   sail ; ʿ
That ill wind may not touch the wing that bears the Holy
   Grail.
And far away to the misty West the mighty cloud is tossed ;
Rent by the wind and shattered till its evil shape is lost.
And now the Northern Glory shines brighter than earthly
   light,
Chaste and pure as the winter stars and as the noon sun bright.
Anon they see in the distance, towering sheer and tall,
Higher than highest home of kings, the bright and gleaming
   wall,
And they cross where the ocean-river their shipmate swept away,
And the ship's bows strike against the strand that is not earthly
   clay
And as she strikes, her timbers start each away from each,
That hardly, springing from her side, her crew the steps may
   reach.
But One there stood upon the steps and saved them from the
   wave :
Mildred and those eleven men.   And unto each He gave

Greeting ; and led them up the steps that pierced the walls of
     ice ;

And up those blessed wanderers went, right into Paradise.

But the wind brought back the story that we have kept so
     long,

And then the caves began again, and sang again the song.

Then silent the drop of the river, on with the river, rolled,

And I stood still and pondered o'er the story he had
     told.

But the river flowed now through meadlands where grazed the
     drowsy kine,

And the slanting sun had traced a walk like a stream of red
     gold wine,

And out of the midst of the ripples, where they were touched
     with light,

There came the sound of a tender song, soft and yet clear and
     bright :

And I knelt down by the margent to catch the words of the
     song,

Else drowned in the kiss the faint wind gave the reeds as it
     went along ;

And the singer stopped in his journey, nor passed along with
     the flood

That beat in the veins of the river like the throbs of a giant's
     blood.

And these were the words that he sang me :

The noon was passed as now,
And the sun aslant in the westward yearned but to cool his
    brow,
Bathed in the lapping waters of the far-reaching sea ;
And I basked in the warmth of the afternoon, I and the wild
    waves free ;
And two there sat on the long low beach, two sisters, side by
    side,
And looked out over the giant sea that knoweth his bounds
    and his tide.
And lo ! one said to other : 'Now tell me, sister mine,
What legend telleth the ocean ? In smiles or in tears of brine
He singeth a song, and its burden is one from day to day,
The same and the same for ever till Time shall pass away.
So have I read ; and I hear him ; yet the meaning I cannot
    tell.'
And she wistful looked across the sea that she feared and
    loved so well.
And her the other answered, 'I have hearkened unto his
    word :
The same when the wind is sleeping as when his roar is
    heard.
Nor have I fathomed his meaning. Yet this flows in on me,
When I stand alone upon the shore and look out over the sea,
That withouten voice or language he sayeth for ever and aye ;
"I am the same throughout all time : I give and I take
    away."'

And they lapsed again into silence, and the sun dropped into
 the waves,
And the dusky shades of the even came out of their hollows
 and caves,
Where they had lurked through the daytime, and hidden themselves from the sun ;
And another night fell on the land, and another day was done.

And I passed along in my rovings, and wandered far and
 wide,
But I came again when the selfsame shore was washed by the
 hundredth tide ;
And a schooner rode at her anchor within the horns of the bay ;
And I dashed myself against her bows and flew up her side in
 spray.
‘Whence came she?’ I asked of a brother, ‘and why is she
 anchored here?’
And he spake in a merry laughing tone, and his voice was
 bright and clear.
‘She came with her sails from the seaward, like a swan with his
 wings of snow,
And she furled her sail and she anchored, now some good
 moon ago ;
And they lowered a boat to the water, and manned her with
 stalwart crew,
And one stepped in with princely mien, and toward the shore
 they drew,

And left her here at her anchor ; and every eve on the beach,
Close to the waves and hardly beyond the breakers' reach,
That tall and princely stranger walks long with one I have
    seen
For many a year, with her sister, look over the waters green :
Eva the fair and lovely, with her flowing, light brown hair.'
And I said, ' Is it she ? I know her. Indeed, she is passing
    fair.
Yet seemeth me her sister is lovelier still than she,
With those deep, wonderful, dark eyes.' And he said, ' It well
    may be.
And, indeed, her eyes look piteous when she cometh down
    alone,
And to the sky and the ocean she maketh her secret moan.'
And I asked, ' Doth she love the stranger ? ' and he answered,
    ' Nay, indeed.
But, alack ! she loveth her sister ; and it maketh her soft heart
    bleed
To think that he will take her, and that she will be left alone.
But she hides her grief within her heart, and keeps it all un-
    known,
And seemeth bright to her sister and maketh her bridal
    dress ;
Nor is there sign that in her soul were aught but happiness.'
And even while he was speaking there came down towards the
    bay
A glad and stately company that stretched in long array

A furlong inward o'er the fields that bordered on the main,

All dight in snowy vesture the ladies of the train ;

And the warm sun upon them shone with a golden hue

As they trooped over the pleasant fields and towards the shore
    they drew.

And in the midst the bridegroom walked proudly with his
    bride,

Whom he shall bear in his good ship across the ocean wide.

Then, following them, her maidens came modestly along,

And there her sister Gwendolen walked tallest of the throng.

But when they came down to the beach worn smooth with
    many a tide,

A tear trembled in Eva's eye that she left her father's side,

Yet through her tears of parting shone a deep, holy bliss,

But he, in his arms he took her, and gave her a farewell kiss.

Then slowly loosed her from him.   'Farewell,' he said, 'and be

As good to him who takes thee now, as thou hast been to
    me.'

Then turned she to her sister, and said, ' O sister mine,

Remember me in the coming years when I am over the brine.

Nor think, whatever my fortune, wherever I shall be,

I shall forget the happy days that I once spent with thee.'

And Gwendolen made answer, ' O sister, when I stand,

As we have stood together oft, alone upon the strand,

How can I else but think of thee ?   I to the sea will say

What once I could have said to thee whom his waves bear
    away.'

But Eva said, ' O Gwendolen, how can I leave thee here?
In winning bliss I leave thee lone.'   But she said, ' Sister dear,
I have the sea and the sea birds, I shall not feel alone ;
Look not back on your sister as on one you have left to moan,
For oft alone have I wandered, and talked with the mighty
    sea;
And, for I know that you are glad, my heart will lighter be.'

Now Eva stands on the good ship's deck, and the boat is
    stowed away.
And they rouse the anchor from its sleep, and the winds in the
    broad sails play.
And there come three long cheers from the beach and they
    send three back again,
And away they draw with a steady breeze straight out into the
    main.
But Gwendolen, with all the rest, turned back and left the sea,
And the marriage guests they spent that night with feasting
    and with glee.
But after dark was fallen she stole down to the shore
Where late had been the parting.   And the sea was cold and
    hoar,
But seemed there a mighty friendship that beat within his
    breast,
A kindness unto all things—a calm in his most unrest,
A depth unmeasured by any man under the waves that roll,
A troubled front, but a stillness for ever within his soul.

And she spoke to the Ocean, saying, ' O playmate, O friendly
    sea,
I am left, I am very lonely—O Ocean, comfort me.'
There came no words from the Ocean, but he seemed to her
    heart to say,
' I am the same throughout all time : I give and I take away.'

And the wind blew over that bare, low shore, nine long and
    deedless years ;
And dark-eyed Gwendolen lived on with but such hopes and
    fears
As come to those who live so still, and watched the ships
    go by ;
And all those years I tarried there to watch her gentle eye.

But a storm three nights blew on that shore, such as there had
    not been
In the memory of living man, and churned to white the green ;
And a tall ship drove on the land and stood fast on the shore.
Like wolves upon a dying elk the waves leapt on her sore,
Tearing and rending hungrily.   Three hours stood she so,
Three mortal hours, while the crew clung to her, and the
    snow
Of foam-flakes drifted past them, under, round them, overhead,
And the restless waves kept leaping up as ravening to be fed ;
Till her timbers parted, and she broke asunder where she stood;
And the crew were in the surges mid the masts and splintered
    wood.

In the morning, when the storm-wind left the sea to sink to
    rest,
One lay upon the shingly beach, bound to an oaken chest.
And dark-eyed Gwendolen came down to watch the swelling
    sea,
And on the beach she found that one, as pale as pale may be :
A little maiden lovely, with flowing light brown hair,
Cold, cold as marble, or as death, and as white marble fair.
And Gwendolen unbound her, and musing sighed : 'Oh me !
Far is it to my father's home, over the long flat lea.'
Then gently she upraised her and bore her toward her home,
Over the seeming endless lea, and left the ocean's foam.
And her dark eyes kept flashing, now on across the plain,
And now upon the maiden, and now toward home again.
At last she gained her father's home, and standing in the door
She found an ancient dame and staid—of eighty years and
    more,
Who came and took the little maid ; and through the door
    they went :
And Gwendolen and that old dame used all their art, and spent
Their skill to bring the life-blood back, nor spent their skill in
    vain ;
For soon, laid in a warm, soft bed, her pulse beat on again.
And when her strength was now enough to answer—this I
    know,
From breezes that sigh round the place, and winds that come
    and go—

Then Gwendolen asked, saying, 'Who are your parents dear?'
For in her heart she knew it was her own niece lying here.
'They both were with me in the ship, I know not where they be,'
She said : 'They lashed me to the chest, and cast me in the
    sea.
For the salt waves swept all the deck, and the planks were
    breaking fast ;
But I remember nothing more of all the sea and blast.'
Then Gwendolen put up her hand and wept a little space :
'Who were they? and whence came they, sweet?' she asked ;
    and o'er her face
Bent tenderly. 'I do not know,' she said ; 'but yesterday
My mother drew me close, and showed me where the flat shore
    lay,
And said there she was born, and there she left a sister dear.
I never heard her voice again.' And from her eye the tear
Rolled down her cheek. 'And even then the wind was fierce
    and high.
They took me down into the ship, the lightning made me cry ;
And then—and then an awful sound; the crew and sea were
    mad.
And then they lashed me to the chest'—and Gwendolen was
    sad.
Then breaking forth she said, 'I am your mother's sister, dear.
O dearest niece, in losing much you win a little here.'
With that she fell upon the bed and clasped her to her breast ;
And in a sweet, long, tender kiss, their lips together pressed.

Then Gwendolen sat thoughtful; she mused on the hidden
    lore
That lay beneath in the ocean, deeper than waves or roar :
The soundless voice of his being, and still he seemed to say :
' I am the same throughout all time : I give and I take away.'

And thus his story ended ; his soft voice died, I ween ;
And I rose and looked across the meads that had smiled so
    bright and green.
But the sun had dropped from the heavens long ere the tale
    was told,
And the moon was up o'er the meadows like a shield of heated
    gold.
But as I watched in the evening she rose up into the sky
Till she shone like a shield of silver.   And cold did her pale
    beams lie
On the land, like a flood of crystal, or like that glassy sea
Before the throne of the Highest.   But a voice came unto me,
That rose from the river, crying :

                  Lo ! what though the moon shine bright ?
There is no warmth in her shining to cheer the cheerless night.
Now hark while I tell you the story of my father's father, the
    sea :
The ancestor of the rivers,—and an agèd man is he.
And they bring down the fruits of the mountains and feed his
    ancient flood,
But 'tis he hath given them being, and in their veins is his
    blood.

Like the changing wind is the ocean to those who see but his
  face ;
Now young and glad, as when Venus rose with her peerless
  grace ;
And now the hoary fleeces flow over his wrinkled cheek,
As when the tall ship founders and the seas close over her
  beak.
For he plays with the breezes, but buffets the storm till he flees
  away :
A hero with the hero, and a playmate with the gay.
But thrilling through and through him, from his face to his
  heart and soul,
Is a love and a hopeless sweetness, a passion that sways the
  whole.
Let the wind be roaring his loudest, or sunk in a deathlike
  swoon,
Still the ocean, the changeless lover, follows the changeful moon.
But she above in the night-time unmoved looks down on his
  love,
Like a god and less than human, as she sits on her throne
  above.
And now she watches his yearning, and now she hides away,
And turns her bright face from him, that worships the Lord of
  Day.
But, seen or unseen, he loves her, and follows her round the
  world ;
And vainly he stretches toward her, with his silvery locks and
  curled ;

And his great heart moves within him, and he heaves a mighty
    sigh ;
And thus for ever and ever he worships his Queen on high.

And he wept as he sang of his father, at the tale of his hopeless
    love ;
And he dived and hid from the moon's cold rays, who shone
    so clear above.

    Lo ! these are the songs of the river; the songs that were
        sung to me :
    The songs of those wandering children sprung from the
        winds and sea.

THE LAST OF HIS KIN.

My heart is glad my breast within :
I am the last of all my kin ;
 For year by year hath seen them fall,
 Like autumn leaves that are the pall
The lifeless earth doth wrap her in.

It is a race with no one now,
Each one hath ploughed—and ceased to plough.
 Yet still in this wise am I vext :
 I sigh, ' Ah me ! 'Tis my turn next :
I cannot live for aye, I trow.'

THE HORSELESS HORSEMAN.

As I walked alone on a moonlit road
Where the kine to the moonbeams sighed and lowed
   And the wind above in the branches spoke,
Methought I heard, 'mid the leaves that stirred,
   A sound as it were of a croak.

And I knew since St. Patrick slew the snakes
There's not been a venomous thing in the brakes.
   But I heard again that sound as I strode :
There are no frogs in old Ireland's bogs,
   And there's not such a thing as a toad.

So I turned to spy out what it might be,
And there I saw, on the swampy lea,
   A man who was sitting, with never a chair,
Up from the ground, in a mantle wound,
   And he seemed to be sitting on air. .

And his legs, as a charger he gripped to ride,
Were parted.   Thought I, he must be astride
    Of a horse that is neither of flesh nor of blood.
A shadowy steed he sure must need,
    For a mortal would sink in the mud.

And I looked at the man in the empty air,
Who seemed to be sitting on never a chair,
    And I tried to look at his unseen horse ;
And I thought that the fowl must be the Diaul
    A-running away with a corse.

When I faced about and looked at the man,
The unseen charger started and ran ;
    And his unseen hoofs from the flints struck light,
And away did he race at a dare-devil pace
    Till the whole was lost in the night.

I've heard the shriek of the weird Banshee,
Telling a soul from earth must flee,
    But never before have I had such a fright,
Nor shook in my shoon ; though I've seen the moon
    Look through the Phooka white.

And now I pray when I walk at night
May I never be cursed with another such sight.
    Oh ! I'll never forget how that phantom ran :
How his feet when dashed on the boulders clashed :
    That riding, horseless man !

L'AMOUREUX.

Who preaches one heart is for one,
  Must know, alas, his own heart small.
No lack of beauties sees the sun :
  My heart is large enough for all.

Threescore and ten the years of men—
  The years of women are as many,
But lovely ladies have, I ken,
  A scant thrice five—few more, if any.

Oh ! bring me in her loveliest prime,
  Her sweetest years, each maiden fair :
The true heart groweth every time,
  A new love's added to its care.

A PARADOX.

Who dares deny that this is true :
  The whole is more than all its parts ?
A whole love than divided love ;
  Or than half love from fifty hearts?

Yet who dare either this deny :
  The part is more than is the whole ?
That treasures halved with one dear love
  Are more than doubled to the soul ?

REGINA MEA.

O BEAUTIFUL Queen,
    Before thy footway,
    Down in the mire, my mantle I lay.
  O merciless One, with eyes as the eyes above
That can be tender though keen,
    Low in the mire I lay
    My life, my love before thy footway :
  Go dryshod over my love !

THE LONELY LADY.

THE lady walked by the sapphire sea
   That kisses the shore
   For evermore
Round smiling Italy—

The lonely lady, in fair weed dight—
   And looked afar where sea and sky
   Still kiss and die.
The sun was bright,
But the lady's hair was as dark as night.

'O lady most like the cypress trees,
What hopest thou from beyond the seas?'
   And she answered, keeping her gaze afar
   Most like a star,
'A hope that shall give my heart its ease.'

Many a wooer
  Had wooed in vain ;
But never a truer
   Loved ever maiden,
    Than he who had left her sorrow-laden
   Yet with living hope, for the boundless main.

Still she gazed o'er the tideless blue,
  Paler day by day.
Over the waves a good ship drew :
Stepped from the gunwale that lover true :
  Still she looked far away.

He stood before her ;
  He spoke her name.
Can words implore her ?
   Can flame wake flame ?
    She looked afar, where sea and sky
    Meet and kiss and, kissing, die.

Love to the loveless ?   Life to the dead !
  Vain all pleadings, hope now vain !
She did not mark his broad sail spread,
As away he sped
  Back o'er the main.

Still she gazed o'er the tideless blue,
    Paler day by day,
And ever around her the seabirds flew.
    Till from where to the deep sea stoops the sky
    To give and to feel one kiss and die,
        All she had watched for came :
        Rest without thought or name ;
        And kissed her life away.

SONNET.

BEAUTY beloved, in its early bloom,
    Surpassing sweet, can tell of love more sweet
    And of pure, passionate thoughts and strength to meet
The untried world.   May my Love's spirit illume
Such beauty as its own.
               But yet a gloom
    Falls on me thinking than her life more fleet
    That visible beauty, worn beneath those feet
That crumble up grey bones within the tomb.

And yet again, the scars of gallant fight
    We prize and honour.   And in coming years
    Shall we not love the record of past tears,
        And ruin won in victory ; and hold
The dear face dearest still ? Young hearts are light ;
    And while a heart can love it is not old.

THE YOUNG YEAR.

THE year is young, and so are we ;
  Not yet have showed the flowers :
And still the wind goes whistling free
  Through all the hawthorn bowers.

But though the flowers are not here,
  And scarce a bud is peeping,
Yet think not this a flowerless year :
  Belike they are but sleeping.

The year is young, and so are we ;
  And love is like the flowers :
And warm and true our love will be
  For all these loveless hours.

THE WAYFARERS

I AND Hope rode side by side :
    I was young and she was fair.
What feared I what might betide ?
I saw the world stretched far and wide,
    By the light of her golden hair.

Love came riding by that way :
    I was young and she was fair.
'Come turn and ride with me, bright fay.'
She said not Yea, she said not Nay,
    But tossed her golden hair.

She rode right on and passed me by :
    I was young and she was fair.
And I left sweet Hope with a bitter sigh ,
And I followed Love, I know not why :
    Followed her golden hair.

Oh ! why would Love not turn with me,
    Turn with her youth so bright and fair,
And ride with Hope on over the lea ?
I and Hope, and Love, all three,
    By the light of their golden hair—

Ride on till Hope could change her name,
    Though always young and always fair,
Another Hope, but yet the same,
And light the coming time with the flame
    Of her beautiful, golden hair?

WILL O' THE WINDMILL.

WHERE the thistledown was blown, love,
    All about the windy wold,
There the miller met a maid, love,
    In the merry days of old.
With her milking-pail, a-singing
    As she sought the meadows sweet,
He met her from the windmill,
    Met her where the two ways meet.
        Singing, 'Will ye, will ye, won't ye,
           Will ye come along with me?
        For they ca' me Willie Windmill,
           O' the mill upon the lea.'

Saying, 'Stay, my pretty milkmaid,
    I have seen thee many a day,
And it warms my heart to see thee,
    Yet takes a' my mirth away.'

Then spake the maiden gaily:
   ' If thy heart be warm enow,
There's muckle mirth upon the earth
   For such a man as thou.
      For you sing your " Will ye, won't ye,
        Will ye come along with me ? "
      And there's many a maid that would,
        If more wouldna', wed with thee.'

' Now, I care not who would wed me,
   Nor who wouldna', lass, I trow ;
Save but she have thy milking-pail,
   And be such an one as thou.
The windmill works for me, lass,
   And I work for the mill ;
And both shall work for thee, lass,
   If thou canst love thy Will.
      Then tell me, will ye, won't ye,
        Will ye come and marry me ? '
      She wouldna' say she will'dna'
        Willie's wedded wife to be.

SO FEATLY IT BEFELL.

'But who,' quoth she, 'will bake and brew,
If I leave home to wed with you?'
    A-standing by the well.
'Why, you shall brew! why, you shall bake!'
Quoth ready Robin—'for my sake.'
    So featly it befell.

'You want two arms,' quoth she, 'I find.
Go, use your own; and that's my mind.'
    His team stood munching slow.
'If you'll not bake,' quoth he, 'nor brew;
Why, do not, lass: I'll still love you.'
    She had her pitcher to go.

'But, Robin, platters would be bare.'
'But, Pattie, even then we'd share.'
    A-standing by the well.
'If you will love, come smooth or rough,
My Robin, love is all enough.'
    So featly it befell.

THE WINTER MOON.

GLOOMY, gloomy looms the night,
And cold are the flakes of wayward light
    That come from the icy moon
Who up in the cloudy space above
Sits giving light, withholding love,
    In night's deserted noon.

And if the moon be lovers' guide,
Who in her loneliness doth ride,
    How cold their love must be !
That blushless maiden, cold and grey,
Who colder grows in redder day—
    Is she love's Deity ?

Old, till we know not of her birth,
Cold as the snowy peaks on earth
    Is she who sails above.
Rather the sun, whose mighty glow
Gives life to all that lives below,
    Should guardian be of love.

ENDYMION.

In the first sweet hours of night
  Sleeping did Endymion lie ;
Flushed with love Selene bright
  Stole betwixt the earth and sky.

Now she stooped and now she stayed,
  Warmed by love and chilled by fear ;
Standing by his side, afraid,
  Blushed she in the evening clear.

There she stood, her cheeks aglow
  Gazing on him longingly.
' Ah ! ' she mused, ' He must not know
  How my love has mastered me.

' Sleep, sweet boy, henceforth alway :
  Know no more of pain or bliss.'
Then she kissed him as he lay ;
  But he never felt the kiss.

F 2

NARCISSUS.

Love-lorn and weary, through the hot midday
  Pale Echo sat amid her rocks and caves,
And sitting watched Narcissus where he lay
  Close where a cold blue stream rolled his waves.
Thoughtless of her he let the hours go by,
But she for very love was near to die.

She longed to tell her woe in plaintive song,
  But cruel Herê's curse forbade her this :
She oft in talk had held the Goddess long
  While Zeus was stealing many a secret kiss ;
Until the Queen of Heaven found out the cheat,
And doomed that she should speak but to repeat.

So now she haunts in caves and must reply
  To every uncouth churl who cares to call,
And say what he says ; give the lie the lie,
  Give fair for fair, and foul for foul to all ;
But not a word may speak of her own mind,
So in unspoken sorrow now she pined.

But he was loved eke by another maid
    Whose love unanswered now had turned to hate,
Who now to dreadful Nemesis had prayed,
    To make him love unloved and feel the fate
He wrought on others ; and in her despair
With many a passionate sigh she mixed the prayer.

And Echo hears the Goddess speak his doom,
    To love the likeness of himself alone ;
And to her cheek hope brings again the bloom
    Thence so long exiled.   For his gentle tone
None can repeat as she ; and now she feels
That one word said by him her sorrow heals.

And now at last he sings, a simple lay,
    Telling of little but a happy life
Where Youth had quite forgotten Love, away
    Beyond the hills where comes there never strife
But Echo straightway answers him ; he hears,
And through him dart a thousand hopes and fears.

With trembling voice he speaks, his lovely eyes
    Full of strange pleadings, 'Speak again, sweet voice
Yet tell not where a loveless region lies,
    But where Love reigns.   Thou art my only choice.
Unloving I have lived and would have died ;
But now I die of love, if you but chide.

' Nay, mock me not,' he cried, for every word,
　　Whatever her will, the nymph must still repeat :
' Nor charge me with that loveless song you heard :
　　I who loved lovelessness now feel Love's heat :
He burns my soul and wastes my strength away,'
But she cries back whatever he may say.

Now hastily he draws near where the stream
　　Spreads from its bed into a little lake
Where he may wade across.　Love-lustrous beam
　　His eyes, his heart beats quicker for her sake ;
And now upon the brink she sees him stand ;
But lo ! he stops still there upon the strand.

Yes, on the mirrored surface of the pool
　　His image floats ; and flushed with love, he sees
Such beauty down beneath the waters cool,
　　That he forgets the voice that erst could please :
Forgets to love his voice, his beauty found ;
And but to win one kiss had fain been drowned.

But when he stoops, and with his outspread arms
　　Would reach the phantom that then comes toward him,
He breaks the water's surface ; and the charms
　　Imprisoned there are shattered and grow dim ;
Till, sick at heart with unfulfilled desire,
He learns to calmly bear an inward fire.

And mute as stone he stands and pines away ;
   While Echo, who must answer every sound
That meets her ear, no single word may say
   To win him back : so straightly is she bound.
If he but spoke she could reply ; but No :
He gazes silent on that face below ;

Until, love-slain, his gentle soul is sped,
   For who could long endure that inward flame ?
And from his snow-white corse first sprang, 'tis said,
   The snow-white flower that still bears his name.
But Echo faded with her grief until
Her voice alone was left to haunt the hill.

DAPHNE.

Now, while my thoughts in Tempe's vale yet stray,
   Of Daphne's cruel fate I fain would sing,
And how her happy hours were taken away.
   O Muse, I need thee, that my verse may ring
   Melodious : Help me ! Teach me how the King
Of Day, arousing Cupid's envious spite,
Brought woe upon himself and that fair sprite.

Lo ! When the Python by his arrows slain
   Lay low, in triumph walked the God of Day ;
And quitted now the blood-drenched battle plain,
   Where stretched in hideous length the serpent lay ;
   And o'er the hills walked proudly on his way,
Thinking no God a nobler fight had won,
Nor any greater deed had e'er been done.

Now Cupid soon he spies, with blade in hand,
   Unto a bow shaping a trusty tree,

Wherewith he might subdue to his command
   · The new-made peoples ; and with covert glee
   His bright eyes twinkled the white chips to see
Fly as he cut : 'With but this little bow,'
Quoth he, ' I mean to lay all nations low.'

'Do what you will,' quoth Phœbus, ' and subdue,
   If so you list, these puny mortal folk !
Such warfare were well fitted unto you,
   And such as these fit subjects for thy yoke.
   But speak not unto us whose deadly stroke
There is no living being can feel but dies :
Yea, thou mayest see where even the Python lies.'

Whom answered Cupid quickly : ' Though you boast
   Your victory over an unreasoning snake,
And scorn my sway that touches every coast
   Where mankind dwells ; yet know that I can shake
   Even immortal natures and can take
Away thy peace—thy peace, thou God of Day :
Vaunt as thou wilt, o'er thee too I hold sway !

Scorning, Apollo left him, ' Let those bear
   The stinging arrows, who can guide their flight,
Sent from a bow with strength enough to tear
   The scaly armour. For thine utmost might,
   If true thy aim, would need a bow too slight,

Therefore fling by thy weapons, wield thy torch !
Thy power is not to kill, 'tis but to scorch ! '

The bow is finished.   From his quiver he takes
    Two arrows, one tipped with pure gold and keen,
The other dull and leaded.   Now he makes
    Straight for Parnassus' top, and there unseen
    Strings his new bow.   The winged shafts, I ween,
Fit well the string, and now they each have flown ;
And Cupid watches as he sits alone.

The gold-tipped arrow in Apollo's heart
    Is buried deep, and in a sudden flame
The God is wrapped ; he feels love's burning smart,
    And with fond words calls upon Daphne's name ;
    Stung with the memory of his boast, and shame
At Cupid's triumph, yet powerless but to yield,
Mad with desire he searches wood and field.

But she, alas, guiltless of any wrong
    Must suffer for the God's disdain of love ;
And walking fearless the still groves along,
    The leaden arrow strikes her from above.
    She falls, as falls beneath the hawk a dove
Struck to the earth.   She pales with new-taught fear,
Yet fearing, knows not any danger near.

But now, by absence but inflamed the more,
　　Apollo comes, and still as death she lies :
She knows her danger now.　And if before
　　She trembled, feels, and almost hopes, she dies,
　　When, with a hungry longing in his eyes,
She hears him call her name and wildly plain
How he has searched the woods for her in vain.

But now, almost already within reach,
　　Where in the brake she hides, the God of Song
Sees her ; and, startled, thus with earnest speech
　　Begins : ' O Maiden, I have sought thee long.
　　Fear not for any ill : I do no wrong.'
For as he spoke she rose to fly—' No, stay ! '
But she in fear sped through the woods away.

He follows.　Now begins a desperate chase :
　　Than she, no hare runs swifter from the hound,
But swifter than the hare's Apollo's pace.
　　No unused feet are his to spurn the ground.
　　Through bush and briar she plunges at a bound.
He follows easier where she breaks her way,
And thus assails her ears with prayers to stay.

' O nymph, O maiden, who is it you flee ?
　　Look on me, am I hateful to the sight ?

You have not seen me.   Lo ! I am not he
  Who feeds the flocks, in sorry weeds bedight.
  I rule rich Delphi and Parnassus' height ;
Me Delos' rock and countless isles obey,
My Sire is Jove himself, my realm the Day.'

Heedless she fled.   Scratched by the shrubs, that soon
  Will be her sisters, and her garment torn,
She flies the God.   Athirst and nigh to swoon,
  She leaves the wood where, through the cruel thorn,
  She makes a way for both ; and now is borne
Swift o'er the grass on trembling feet.   While he
Pursues her still though silent now as she.

Ah, luckless maid !   How perfect showed her form
  Bared by the wind that blew her garment back,
Tattered to shreds.   But ruthless as a storm
  Chasing a cloud, he pressed upon her track.
  She feels his hot breath now, ' Alack, Alack,'
She cries, ' Father Peneus, not with thee
Can I now rest : I can no further flee !

' I cannot reach thy waves ; but grant me this,
  Against thy daughter's prayer stop not thine ears,
This is my utmost hope, I ask not bliss,
  Yet let me win this comfort for my tears :
  Let me be but a tree that nothing fears,

A thoughtless tree that only lives, and knows,
If naught of happiness, still naught of woes.'

Her prayer was heard ; and as the God embraced
   With eager arms the trembling nymph, and deemed
His love fulfilled, already her feet were laced
    In the firm ground ; her tears dried as they streamed ;
    She stiffened in his arms, while dark leaves gleamed
Instead of hair, her arms to boughs had grown ;
Apollo stood by a bay tree alone.

But still with eager lips the bark he kissed,
   And thus he cried, 'Through the revolving year
Keep thy green leaves ; and thou shalt ever list
    To the sweet tones of music, O most dear
    Of trees ; lo, thou my lyre that sounds so clear
Shalt ever wreath, and wreath my hair and bow,
That thee I love all men and Gods may know !

.

THE SCULPTOR.

O LADIES nine, so often called in vain,
　　Who often come uncalled, and hidden raise
　　Immortal music in the poet's lays
Who weens his own not yours the lovely strain,
　Come unto me, yet take from me that sin :
　　Mine are the earthly blots, to you all praise,
　If any, for the rhymes I here begin.

For of such sin I tell.　In days of old
　　A Cypriot lived, a man cunning to win
　　From snowy stone the hidden shape within,
Or work in bronze, or ivory and gold.
　He was not loved of men, but rather feared :
They felt he guarded mysteries untold,
　For with strange lines of care his brow was seared.

Now had his city voted there should be
　　A statue made of marble that should show
　　The Cyprian Queen blest, from the Realms below,

With lost Adonis ; and an ample fee
    Had set aside, and called on all who knew
The sculptor's art, or there or over sea.
    So gold and honour were the victor's due.

So many strove. But lo, this sculptor's mind
      Nigh lifelong on the story chosen had dwelt
      With thought and longing till he almost felt
The conquering passion Love's own Queen could bind.
And to that laughter-loving Goddess kind
    Untiringly had prayed, and to the Nine
    Till they had touched his soul with art divine.

For Venus sent a maid across his ways,
    As fair as morning light the hills above,
    Who all unconscious taught his heart to love,
Till in deep ponderings he spent his days,
    And pale he grew. For so the Goddess willed ;
    She held him back from happiness fulfilled,
That he might work his work unto her praise.

And so the work grew on, wrought out in pain
    As beauty ever is wrought, till it could tell
    Of grace divine that on the maker fell,
And of a heart not passion-fraught in vain.
    'Twas well for them the citizens should raise
    A noble statue in the goddess' praise.
For him, what thought had he of glory or gain ?

And ever as the end approached more near
  New depths of love welled up within his breast,
  And all in marble his great art expressed,
Passion and tender love and awful fear.
  For Venus drew the maiden's guileless heart
Slowly to his that he might know full clear
  All worlds of love, hope, doubt, delight, and smart.

So now at last, sweeter than utmost thought
  He knows fulfilment of united loves—
  The maid is his.   The Goddess of the Doves
By bliss now teaches what by pain she taught.
  For nothing can be wholly taught by woe,
  Nothing by joy alone ; hence mingled flow
Their waters here in our life-valley caught.

And now at length the statue is achieved :
  A miracle, half human, half divine.
  The stone, long buried lifeless in the mine,
Even the undying Thought wherewith once heaved
  The bosom of Venus fitly may enshrine.
  The hand of man might crush the marble cold,
  But not the Thought its silent wonders hold.

Another sculptor in that city dwelt,
  A goodly man with store of wealth untold,
  Pleasant of speech and lavish of his gold ;

Him men loved well, and many fawning knelt
For favours to him, nor would he deny.
    Within his mansion all men might behold
His *Venus and Adonis* set on high.

Right craftily 'twas fashioned and most fair,
    With true proportions.   Many a man had he
    Set under him, servants both bond and free ;
Though he worked hard himself, and with great care.
    And now his group stands finished for the day
    When dressed in solemn garb and state array
The appointed judges shall their choice declare.

Now when the groups were set up in full view
    These two alone seemed worthy of the prize.
    Then did the well-loved, goodly man arise
And say : 'O fellow citizens, to you
Free would I give the utmost I can do,
    But honour holds me back, for men would say
    I tried with bribery your minds to sway.'

But not a word that other sculptor said.
    He knew how utterly his wondrous art
    Surpassed the other's.   Still he stood apart
And waited for the judgment to be read.
    The herald then declared, with sounding voice,
    That on the rich man's group had fallen their choice.
Whereat the crowd cried 'Aye !' and did rejoice.

G

Careless of gold and fame, but yet enraged
    That such a slight upon his work was thrown,
    The other sought his house, and there alone
Paced up and down, as doth a lion caged.
  He thought of work through many a bygone day,
  He thought of all the subtle depths that lay
    In eye and lip, and cried with bitter tone :

'Ah ! cursèd city, that could thus have sold,
    For the mere glitter of a smiling eye,
    A treasure that once lost no gem could buy !
No ! not the world doth such another hold.'
And now with indignation over-bold
  He cried, ' The gods could not another give !
  I—I alone, can make cold marble live ! '

Angered the Muses heard him, and they flew
    To Aphrodite, laughter-loving Queen.
    But laughter in her looks was not, I ween.
'Ah ! ' cried she.   'What should we for mortals do,
  Who only fling our gifts into our face
  And call them theirs ?   And safely they disgrace
Immortals.   Still their boldness they may rue.'

The Furies now they sent upon the man ;
    Goading his soul to madness, till he knew
    Not what he said nor did ; and haggard grew

His cheek, and deathly pale beneath their ban,
While through his aching head incessant ran
   Tormenting thoughts ; and now a darker thought
   Seized on him : straight his sculpture-room he sought.

There stood the peerless group, brought back at eve.
   He looked at it a long, long look; and then
   Spake thus : ' Be seen no more of gods or men ! '
The chisel is grasped that taught those stone breasts heave
   With love ; stout arms and skilled make labour short.
And ere the Dawn may her bright garment weave
   The work of years is as a dead man's thought.

   ' Lo ! I alone could such a work renew.'
      Thus he began, ' And lest my purpose fail
      Never to grave a statue more, a nail
Shall make impossible what I might do.
      He plucked an iron nail from off the ground,
      Rent through his eyes, then giddy turning round,
Fell in a swoon, and all as nothing grew.

Ah me ! how horrible to rise in night
      Amid the day ! In agony he calls—
      His hollow voice rings hollower through the halls—
He calls for his fair love, his sweet delight.
A slave comes to him ; at the ghastly sight
      Of bleeding eyeballs he exclaims on fate,
      And tells all bad news in his frightened prate.

Alas, another woe?   Where will it end?
    Why have the Gods turned enemies? and why
    Struck this deep wound when she is no more by
Could bind it, and all tender care could lend?
Who now upon your nighted life shall tend?
    But now a sudden anguish seized your wife—
    We could not find you—now she hath not life.'

    spake the slave confusedly, and more.
    The other stood and listened for a while,
    Then came upon his cheek a ghastly smile ;
He turned and felt his way out by the door.
    'The Gods have cursed him : let him go alone.'
    So mused the slave.   And on without a groan
That man once loved of Gods walked, stained with gore.

And so he groped along the white paved street,
    Through the tall city, through the city gate ;
    And though so silent, yet did not abate
His madness, for he shunned all men to meet.
    Shunned help or comfort since cold Dian's bow
    Shot the last shaft that added to his woe ;
    And mad and blind alone he seeks his fate.

THE

MAID OF ARTEMIS

A PLAY

IN FIVE ACTS

DRAMATIS PERSONÆ.

IDMON, *King of Argos*   EVADNE, *Wife to* AGIS

AGIS   PYRRHA, *Daughter to* IDMON

DAPHNIS   IO

MILO   A PRIESTESS OF ARTEMIS

CREON   AN OLD PEASANT WOMAN

A SOLDIER

Soldiers, &c.

Scene in Argolis except for part of Act II. ; for the last Act in the temple of Artemis at Argos.

ACT I.

SCENE I.—*Argolis.   A Forest.*

Enter CREON.

Creon.   I love not this ; and yet slow time bears witness
What the Gods will is best.   Their oracle
Has said, ' No man shall reign in Argolis
Save Pyrrha he devote to Artemis.'
Pyrrha, the daughter of our king, now fled,
Hearing her fate.   And I must track and bring
The living prey to death.   I never saw her,
For still she was immured about the shrine
Of that great Goddess.   But she has been traced ;
For all men marked the raiment that she wore.
One had her ring, exchanged for food.   Here see
One I must question.

Enter Peasant Woman.

Peasant.   Save you, gallant sir !
   Creon.   Gramercy, dame.   Pray have you met in the woods
A maid of gentle nurture ?   In the hunt

Such one was parted from us, and with heed
We seek her.

Peasant.   Here are gentle maids enough,
But none enough gentle to be this maid.

Creon.   Is there a village near ?

Peasant.   La ! never a village ;
But scattered up and down you find the folk.

Creon.   Guide me where I may question others.   See,
You shall not lose your time.   *[Gives money.*

Peasant.   Nor you your bounty !   *[Exeunt together.*

SCENE II.—*In the Forest, before* Io's *Cottage.*

Io *in the doorway.   Enter* Peasant Woman.

Peasant.   How does your brother, Io ?

Io.   Not so well ;
What is there I could do ?

Peasant.   'Tis past my leechcraft,
Though I am reckoned wise.   Knows he your face ?

Io.   I hardly think so.

Daphnis [*within*].   Where was it ?   In the sky ?

Io.   He knows not what he says.

Daphnis [*within*].   When will it be light ?

Peasant.   Why, it is high noon now.   Well, I must on.

If he live not we know not who 'tis dies.
That gold chain he wears hidden—

  Io.   I know well,
And what you tell of it.

  Peasant.   Yes, it was clasped
About his neck when you and he were found,
Two pretty babes, left in the woods.   Why he,
He went on four legs still, the chuck.

  Io.   Well, mother,
I care not whose we are, for twain we found,
Your neighbour and her goodman, who made up
Whatever loss we had.

  Peasant.   Peace be with them !
The good dame showed me how upon his neck,
Crossed by the chain, there was a blood-red mark.
Tis sixteen years gone now.

  Daphnis [*within*]. Io, you leave me ! [*Exit Io into cottage.*

  Peasant. Poor boy! she would not leave you for the world.
Well, I must on.   An open-handed lord
Was that this morn.   What lady did he seek ?   [*Exit.*

     Enter PYRRHA.

  Pyrrha. Now help me, Artemis, for I am yours !
Not at your steps a victim, but instead,
A living maiden of the woods, but yours
No less.   Stay, this is some poor cotter's home,

A safer than a palace.   Pray you, sirs,
Give me to eat.

   Io [*within*].   And welcome, with that voice.
But hush, one here lies sick.   [*Enters.*]   Pardon, sweet lady.

   Pyrrha.   I pray you pardon me.   But I am faint,
And I must tell you, in much danger.   Here,
This bracelet wear, if you will shelter me ;
And yet I think I know enough of eyes
To know this needless.

   Io.   Hide here in the cot
If any follow you.   What is your fear ?

   Pyrrha.   The way men think to serve the gods.

   Io.   Come in,
But softly, pray.   My brother, who is all
The world to me lies sick nigh unto death.

   Pyrrha.   I have some skill, much skill do flatterers say,
In herbs and medicines and antidotes.
Let me but try my craft.

   Io.   Let you ?   Oh ! try it ;
And I would die to serve you should you save him.

                      [*Exeunt into cottage.*

ACT II.

SCENE I.—*The Forest.*

Enter CREON.

Creon.   I cannot wish success, and I must think
Idmon too fearful ; for our men are bold,
As numerous and well practised as the foe's.

Enter Soldier.

Soldier.   My lord, I bring these from my liege the king,
Sent with hot speed.

Creon.   What may this tell me ?

[*Reads.*] 'Creon, most trusted ; whereas we were hard
pressed, we are now beleaguered.   Our general, Butes, in one
battle with Agis, has lost both his army and his life.   What
hope remains to us is fixed upon your known skill in a city's
defence.   Leave, therefore, this necessary quest, and hasten to
us for the dispatch of war's more necessary affairs.

'IDMON, of Argos, king.'

Haste then, much liefer than to hunt this maid
The stricken field !   What ground has gained the foe ?

Soldier.   All ; right from whence he came up to our walls ;
Where camps he though the other side is open.   [*Exeunt.*

SCENE II.—*A room in* AGIS' *home.*

EVADNE *and* MILO *discovered.*

Evadne.   Tell me, stout Milo, how is the field gone ?
All yesterday the sky was muffled up
In frighting darkness.   But how went the field ?

Milo.   To tell you this I came.   Agis, your lord,
Is crowned in Argos.

Evadne.   We should praise his valour
Were he less near than husband.

Milo.   Rather praise
The gods who gave us victory.   For they
Gave it most wonderfully !

Evadne.   How, wonderfully ?

Milo.   Butes then nine days back in open field
Had fallen, as you heard ; and every day,
Pitched by the town, we did assault its walls,
Though still with loss.

Evadne.   Who led ?

Milo.   ˘   Agis himself.
Then in the town of nights the swingeing axe
We heard at work.   Till on the tenth day's fight,

As we drew shattered off, sheer o'er the walls
They shot a bridge of wood.   Then in array
Full fronted, shield to shield, their phalanx swept
Down on our broken ranks.

  Evadne.   And then you rallied,
As when the swarthy bear, driven to bay,
Turns on the dogs?

  Milo.   I saw your lord stand forth
Most like that bear, but with him scarce a man.

  Evadne. And you were with him?

  Milo.   I was.   Onward they came,
In the forefront their king ; while heavy darkness,
Such as you say, weighed down the air.   When lo !
Out of the riven clouds the Gods hurled down
A thunderbolt upon him.

  Evadne.   Oh ! their altars
Shall speak our gratitude.

  Milo.   That was enough ;
The scale was turned, and up the bridge swept we,
Cutting them piecemeal.

  Evadne.   So is Idmon perished !

  Milo. Burnt up until we could not find his corse.

  Evadne. The Gods fulfil their oracles !   But Agis
Stands no more safe.   It said ' *No* man shall reign.'

  Milo. True.

  Evadne.   Then a maid named Pyrrha must we seek.

  Milo. I have it sure King Idmon seven times

Sent with rich gifts if he might sacrifice ·
Another for his daughter.

Evadne. And each time
It was refused?

Milo. The priestess as she spoke,
When Artemis possessed her, steadfastly
On the king's daughter looked. Hence, say the wise,
She is demanded.

Evadne. Then must she be found.

Milo. You would not have her slain?

Evadne. There is a time
For tenderness ; but when my purpose calls,
You know my nature.

Milo. Yes, you sent me forth
With Agis' children by his first sweet wife
To make your boy sole offspring.

Evadne. I did. And you
Returned without them. I will press my lord
To have her sought for. She who would not die
To save her father, dies to save his foe.
I will to Argos now.

Milo. There I should bring you
Where you shall share the crown.

Evadne. I will prepare. [*Exit.*

Milo. If dark deeds make long reigns her king reigns long.
But that last time she plotted, on her camp
Stole the familiar spirit, hooded Death,

She had not reckoned with.   For men with Death
Are like a good-souled tippler with mine host:
See, but scarce heed, until he shows the score,
And must have payment.   Whew ! her plots, and boy
For whom they were, are swept beyond all reach.

ACT III.

SCENE I.—*The Forest.*

Enter PYRRHA *in peasant's clothes, and* IO.

Pyrrha.   I think it must be safe.

Io.   Ten days are gone
Since first you found us.   And our simple folk
Would never dream that you, in such poor weeds,
Could the king's daughter be.

Pyrrha.   And still my father,
Through half the score of years that I have known,
Enshrined me in the temple, till none knew
Of all his court my features.   Not himself
He suffered see me ; but across a screen
Head high we used to talk.   Because he thought
Devoted meant but *given up*, not *slain.*
Till Agis set his face against our peace,
In the first shock successful.   Then in fear
He chose the direr meaning.   Now a change
Of raiment makes me safe.   But you who give it
I cannot thank enough.

Io.   My thanks are yours.
My brother Daphnis, like a heedless boy
Who ventures to a mountain wall's sharp edge
And giddy stands, stood on the verge of life ;
And you were the strong hand that caught him back
Ere he could fall.

Pyrrha.   That so I did delights me,
Both for itself, and for it has unlocked
Your heart to me.   I never in my life
Felt such content as in the woods with you.
I find this gain in loss, that I have found
A friend even by loss.

Io.   Pyrrha, I loved you
Before you saved my brother's life.   The trees
Are dear to me, and dear this air ; and oft
I thought me happy, till you came and taught
How much more ' happy ' meant.

Pyrrha.   I could speak on
For ever of our loves.   But here one comes—
Remember I am *Chloë.*

Enter Peasant Woman.

Peasant.   Good-day, neighbour.
Io and Pyrrha.   Good-day to you.
Peasant.   Your brother is deadly sick.
Io.   Nay, mother, he is healed and gathers strength.

H

Peasant. I cannot see, forsooth. Did this maid heal him?

Io. Yes, mother.

Peasant.   Poisons are burnt out by poison.
Though she has healed him she has made him sick :
Healed body, stricken breast.

   Io.   Peace, mother, peace !

Peasant. The lad is sick ; I saw him walk even now
With head down as the grass were book.   Take care !
Who cures can kill.

   Io.   Peace, mother, he is whole.

Peasant. Well, then, enough of this.   But have you heard
The news they tell to-day?   They say the King
Has lost the day, and wanders in the woods.

   Pyrrha. What ? What say they? Is he . . . you said the
      king—
Heard you no more ?

   Peasant.   Why bless you, gentle maid,
It harms not us.   I reck not much of kings.
But I must on.   Good luck be with your brother.   [*Exit.*

   Pyrrha. I pray this be not true.   He would have taken
My life that he first gave.   So do the Gods,
And yet we love them no one thought the less ;
So I my father no one thought less love.

SCENE II.—*The Forest.*

Enter IDMON *with his eyes bandaged, led by* CREON.

Idmon.   Into what sort of country are we come ?

Creon.   The same deep forest that for five long miles
Has girt us without break.

Idmon.   See you no end ?

Creon.   The trees grow here more scattered

Idmon.   I must rest ;
I will not keep you long.

Creon.   My liege, my life's term !

Idmon.   The Gods doomed, or that bridge you built had
    saved us.
Why did you lead me from the field, when fear
Had bid me stay ?

Creon.   Fear you to live, my liege ?
Now is not when, nor I the man, to teach ;
Yet should you scorn not the great gift of life,
That has been spared you, as it seems to me,
Not by old, shaking Chance.   The God's own hand
Left your soul living though struck off your crown.

Idmon.   We found our empires on the sands of time ;
They are foredoomed to fall.   All men know this,
Yet when the law in his own case holds good

H 2

Each thinks it strange.   But now, most trusted lord,
A blind king cannot win nor wear a crown.
Hence thine allegiance do I will away
To our late foe ; make peace with, nay, more, serve
This king of Argos.

    Creon.   Good my liege, what mean you ?
You know me true.

    Idmon.   True to the soul I know you.

    Creon.   And is not now when I should show my truth ?

    Idmon.   No !   Truth a king needs in his hour of prime,
When untruth dogs him round.   But what man now
Would lie to me ?   This service I retain :
Thou shalt not—not for any hope—reveal
Where I am hid.

    Creon.   My liege, I promise it.

    Idmon.   Well, then, away !   But let me be once more,
Though never more, a king.

    Creon.   [*Kneels.*]   My honoured liege,
I will obey at full.   [*Rising, aside*] But first will watch him,
Till he has found some shelter.   [*Aloud*] Yet this king
Shall not reign long, let but the Fates keep trust !

    Idmon.   He cannot slay my daughter.   Would to Zeus
I had her now.   We do but double loss,
Striving with fate ; but I am justly paid.
I had a treasure more than kingdom's worth,
And I . . . well, leave me here.

Enter DAPHNIS, *musing*

Creon.   This boy looks simple.
Prithee, good youth, care for this stricken lord
Till you shall hear from me.   In the meantime
This shall requite your pains.
   Daphnis.   Good sir, I will.
If you would find him, yonder through the trees
You see my home.
   Creon.   Farewell.
   Idmon.   Find better fortune. [*Exit Creon.*
   Daphnis.   My lord, what ails your eyes?
   Idmon.   Nothing, boy, ails them,
More than aught ails the dead.   The lightning touched them,
And they are not.   Greater lights quench the less.
What are these coming?

Enter PYRRHA *and* IO.

   Daphnis.   My sister and a friend.
   Pyrrha.   I know my father's voice.   Io, now feign
That I am dumb ; because he too knows mine,
And he may hate me.   Could I not have died
To save him?
   Daphnis.   Io, for this honoured lord
We must make such home as our home can be.

Io.   I and my brother, with one who has lost
All speech, live some steps hence, where food and shelter
Are yours whileas you will.

    Idmon.   The Gods requite you.
I pray you, boy, you lead me by the hand.   [*Exeunt.*

ACT IV.

SCENE I.—*The Forest, before* Io's *Cottage.*

Enter DAPHNIS, *musing.*

Daphnis.   I do not know who gave to me my life,
For I was found under the greenwood tree.
Yet Lady Pyrrha gave to me my life,
Who saved it.   I were graceless not to love her ;
Yet with how much more than that love, I love her.
Fie, fie !   She is the daughter of a king :
And I—they found me lying in the woods :
Under an oak that is the forest's king,
The son then am I of the forest's king !
O tricky heart that would beguile the head,
Alas, how little do your wiles bested !
Here Pyrrha comes whose presence slakes my pain—
To make it burn the fiercer ; I'll away.
And yet in absence is my only gain,
To love her more and more from day to day.   [*Exit.*

Enter PYRRHA *and* IO.

Io.   You lose the gentle hand of courtly ease
To find rough faring.
  Pyrrha.   It is well exchanged.
Kind was the priestess, yet her kindness fell
But cold and distant ; not like yours, sweet Io ;
But snow upon a frozen summit lone.
  Io.   Our love and not your losses drew me near.
You are still o'er my head.
  Pyrrha.   I wish I were not,
[*Aside*]   Oh, how I wish I were as free as she,
To love, and be loved back where I most love.
Daphnis dares not look up to lowly me
Who hold his lowliness all heighth above.
  Io.   Yet you are sad.   I think you weigh the loss.
  Pyrrha.   I have lost nothing, yet I would gain more.
  Io.   What would you gain ?
  Pyrrha.   The loss of royal birth,
To match my fortunes.   For it is a cage,
However gilded, where the bird may sing,
But never ride in freedom on the wing.
  Io.   I would you would do what you can and sing—
That the young priestess taught you.
  Pyrrha.   Answer me.

[*Sings.*]   Oh the bird is in the cage,
And youth is thrall to age.

Io.   Let be.

Pyrrha.   Who will break the chain,
Set us free again,

Io.   Set us free?

Pyrrha.   King save from his crown,
Lad from learned frown?

Io.   Let be.

Pyrrha.   Let lover, lover wed,
Not long descent instead !

Io.   Set us free.

Pyrrha.   Leave as dead what dies.
Freedom's lore is wise.

Io.   Ah me,
                                                    Set us free !

Pyrrha.   She was of low degree who made that song
And taught me sing it, yet loved a king's son,
Who loved back ; but the king thwarted their hopes,
And she became a maid of Artemis.

Io.   ' King save from his crown ? '   Our king is saved,
And leads these two days such a life as I.
But is it sweet to him?

Pyrrha.   I am to blame,
So long to leave him who is blind.   But Io,
My love of you made me undutiful,
When I should while away his heavy hours.   [*Exit.*

Io.   I wonder how it is men can be found
Who dare be kings.   Or how they have a heart
To do such deeds to be so.   Pyrrha feared,
Because she fled, her father hated her.
But when he on himself reproaches heaped,
Who thought to slay her, she straight who she was
Revealed to him.   Whereat his sudden joy
Showed how he loved her.   Yet to keep his crown,
Her he had rendered up.

Enter DAPHNIS.

Daphnis.   Io, to hiding
With both our guests !   Two officers of Agis
Have tracked our Princess, and this place have ringed
Already with a wall of men.   And one
Who saw the Princess in her flight and knows
Her face, a woodman, have they seized.
     Io.   Tell Pyrrha
To lead her father to the hollow tree :
You with them.
     Daphnis.   Every tree, in trunk and branch,
I saw them search : and like a serpent's coil,
The ring still tightens.
     Io.   Do as I have said.
I in the cot remain and give a story,
How both fled yesternight.   About it !   [*Exit* DAPHNIS

       Thus
And thus. This woodman knows her face and dress ;
If he find either, that is the Princess.
I in her raiment shall be found alone
Here in the cot. Her face being all unknown
Save to one hind, who, I will venture, swears
King's daughter her whoe'er such garment wears,
Makes easy personation.

    Re-enter DAPHNIS, *with* IDMON *and* PYRRHA.

       Pray now, hide !
Trust to my wits.
  Pyrrha.   But, Io, there is danger
In what you plan ; if they should find deceit,
Your life would pay it.
  Io.   Never fear for me.
Quickly away !
  Daphnis. Let me bear danger too !
Sister, you are a churl to give me none.
Let me stay in the cot.
  Io.   No, I am readier ;
Boys always blunder. You shall trust in me.
But now away ! You know that tree we found
Where all could hide. And ere they find you there
I will have led them on false scent.
  Idmon.   How well
You teach me what a father's love should be. [*Exeunt omnes.*

SCENE II.—The Forest.

Enter together the Soldier *and the* Peasant Woman.

Peasant. You cannot be certain of what you have never seen.

Soldier. I tell you, good woman, we are certain, and doubly certain, that there lurks hereabouts she whom we seek.

Peasant. Then are you certain of more than I.

Soldier. We must assault and take every tree ; break our necks climbing, or have our heads broken for not.

Peasant. Well, well, there are men enough, when all is done.

Soldier. Come, mother, if I would be rough I could.

Peasant. It is not of your softness to be rough. You served the Lord Creon. I saw you with him, and you told me who he was.

Soldier. I did, and a good lord to serve.

Peasant. So say I, and a bounteous. But he served our king Idmon, and now you follow this Agis.

Soldier. If I have followed the living king, not died with the dead, I but follow my lord Creon. He now commands us jointly with a right valiant soldier, Milo, the right hand of Agis. This is but talking. Take me where Idmon's daughter hides. Find her we shall ; and what skills it which of us first ?

Peasant. Why, then, sit still and be last.

Soldier. I mean what skills it to her or you? If I find her I have gold for my pains.

Peasant. Then I wish you few pains till they fall in the market.

Soldier. I need not keep all ; and if you have helped find her——

Peasant. You will give me fair share of the nothing that you'll win. I tell you she you seek is not here, or I should know it.

Soldier. Do you doubt our Captain's word?

Peasant. There is none here but a silly, love-sick boy and a blind old man, yet withal young for his age. And two women such as I.

Soldier. Why, you told me a while ago they were young and winsome?

Peasant. And so they are.

Soldier. But so are you not.

Peasant. If you want love-talk, so are you not. ' Such as I ' is ' of no higher estate.'

Soldier. I shall be missed by the Captain ; and then, Marsyas, save my skin better than your own ! Will you not show me at least your winsome wenches?

Peasant. You'll find them yourself, or else you'll find them gone.

Soldier. I waste my time.

Peasant. And mine too.   [*Exeunt severally*

SCENE III.— *The Forest, before* Io's *Cottage.*

Enter MILO, CREON, *and the* Soldier.

Milo.   Climb every tree.   If you can't, cut it down.

[*Exit Soldier.*

I know not how you let that man make off
Who Pyrrha's face had seen.

Creon.   Touch not my care.
The fellow fled, and wisely, for your men
Are not so gentle as to reconcile
The Argives to King Agis.   This I say
Myself, full reconciled.

Milo.   [*Aside*] Too plausible ;
I think him scarce in earnest.   [*Aloud*] Anyway
We know for certain that we close her round.
Why may she not be here?

Creon.   [*Aside*] This is the cot
Where Idmon dwells.   How shall I make him leave it ?
[*Aloud*] I doubt much we have reached her.   Up to here
I tracked her ere I was recalled.

Milo.   Why then,
Here she should be.

Creon.   She would not stay here long ;
She must by now be hence.   You are unwise
To spend our moments in so strait a search
Of here where she is not.

Milo.   Here she is tracked,
And nowhere farther.   She may be in this cot.

Creon.   Well, I will search it.

Milo.   Rather watch outside ;
And if she break out seize her.   [*Aside*] I will trust
My bluntness ere his sharpness.

Creon.   As you will.

[*Milo goes into Io's cottage, while Creon speaks aside.*]

Pray the king be not here.   I see he doubts me,
But doubt me he need not.   Right loyally Idmon
My service had ; and any heir of his
My service should have.   But the land a king
Needs ; hence as I served Idmon, so I serve
Agis, e'en though it bring to death a maid.

Milo.   [*Within.*]   Found !

Enter with Io in Pyrrha's first dress.

                    And in her own raiment undisguised.
This must be she.   We need no woodman here.

Io.   No vassal I to make my royalty.

Milo.   Well, lady, I am hard of mood, and say
At once what I might mince.   Victorious Agis
Would yield the Gods your life.

Creon.   Lady, your father
Doomed you to nothing worse.   But though you perish,
No mean fate stays your breath.   The victim falls
Holy and consecrate.

Io.   Trick not out
Death in fair colours ; for I can endure
To see him in his own.

Milo.   You were a soldier,
Were you a man, whom I would choose to stand
At my right hand in battle.

Io.   Lead now on,
And when I give you cause, that praise unsay.

SCENE IV.— *The Forest.*

Enter DAPHNIS *and* PYRRHA, *meeting.*

Pyrrha. What news?

Daphnis.   When first I stole out from the tree
I crept about the woods, but found no man ;
The soldiers were clean gone.   So to our cot
I ventured, but no Io there I found.

Pyrrha. Then they have borne her off to show the track
She told them I had taken.

Daphnis.   I know not ;
But there are stories how sometimes a maid
Is fairy, and at seasons she is changed
Into a timid doe.   Could these be true,
And Io such an one?

Pyrrha.   Boy, you are wandering,
She has been taken as a guide.
    Daphnis.   No, lady.
It cannot be but she has turned a doe ;
For in the cot is all her raiment heaped.
She's gone and this is left.
    Pyrrha.   That cannot be.   [*Exit.*
    Daphnis. O lady, for my sister I am sad,
But how much sadder if it were for thee !
And yet I dare not love thee.

Re-enter PYRRHA.

    Pyrrha.   Daphnis,
Go to my father.   No, wait while I think.
I found this bracelet on the path, 'twas mine.
Daphnis, you know where lies my courtly garb.
Is it still there ?
    Daphnis.   What is your drift, dear lady ?
    Pyrrha.   No—I must go ; but go you to my father.
    Daphnis.   What shall I tell him ?
    Pyrrha.   Tell him ?   Let me see,
I must piece hints together.   [*Aside*] In my raiment
She has surrendered, but this bracelet dropt
As to the cot she carried what I wore
From where it lay ; where if it lie not now,
My fear is true.   Die for me, Io, more dear

I

Than life ? [*Aloud*] Sweet Daphnis, to my father haste ;
Tell him, till we know more, that Io leads
The hunt astray.

    Daphnis.   Lady, I will.   [*Exit.*

    Pyrrha.   Of this

Must I now satisfy myself at once.   [*Exit.*

———————

SCENE V.—*Another part of the Forest.*

Enter DAPHNIS.

    Daphnis.   Yonder's the hollow tree where Idmon waits,
Till I bring word all's safe.

Enter CREON.

    Creon.   Well met˜for me ! [*Aside.*]
Boy, you are he I left to tend the king—
That blind lord was the king.

    Daphnis.   I know it, sir.

    Creon.   He told you? Well, by his command I served
Agis ; but never breathed himself still lived :
Now must I speak with him.

    Daphnis.   But pray you, sir,
Have you seen one who might my sister be ?
For she is lost.

Creon.   I hope she may be safe,
But now this part was filled with Agis' men ;
I was one leader who was sent to find
King Idmon's daughter, Pyrrha.
    Daphnis.   Would you harm her ?
    Creon. I would not now, could I re-act the past :
But willingly I did.
    Daphnis.   Villain, what harm ?
    Creon. Good boy, you call me true. We found her, seized
And led her where she shall endure the taste
Of bitter death.
    Daphnis.   Villain, the same shalt thou !
Boar-spear to arms and armour in this cause !
Oh, Villain !
    Creon.   Take this message to the king.
Waste not thy honest hate on me, good boy.
Tell him if ever he has known remorse
For that he once devoted her to death,
To save her now : to Argos let him haste,
And there to Agis yield his body up
To buy her life. I dare not meet his eyes,
Nor any man's. When we had Pyrrha sure,
Smote then the damning blackness of our deed,
And wheeling round I left them. In the wood
I left two horses : set the king on one,
And, riding on the other, be before
The sacrificial knife !

Daphnis.   [*Aside*] First Io gone,
And Pyrrha now gone too !   [*Exit.*

   Creon.   While I will wander
An exile from all men except myself,
Myself who juggled so with right and wrong,
That deepest wrong, murder and treachery,
Most crooked reason urged my heart think right.
Pyrrha I chased to make my lord stand firm ;
My lord I left when he no longer stood ;
But evil never yet served country's good.   [*Exit.*

Enter PYRRHA.

   Pyrrha.   All that I wore is gone !   My fear's fulfilled !
True friend, sweet Io, would you die my death ?
But you shall not.   Oh me ! how hard to die !
To near the end of perishing thought, and lose
The free sky, love and friendship ; all whereby
The spirit knew itself ; to leave in midst
Of not yet ended hopes.   Yet this you do
Even to save it me.   Thou shalt not, Io !
I will win back my own death.   If I falter,
I am more base than clay.   Here in the woods
Stand two tall steeds, the hunters left belike.
One will I mount, and when the whizzing air
Sweeps by my brow, fear will not clog my heart.   [*Exit.*

Re-enter DAPHNIS, *leading in* IDMON.

Idmon.   Hasten,   boy !   Lead   me !   Long   have   I   felt
    remorse,
But Creon's makes mine deeper.   With my life
I will redeem hers that I once had spilt
To steady a base crown.
    Daphnis [*looking off*].   He said two horses,
But there is only one.
    Idmon.   Haste, bind me on,
And lead me, ere too late !
    Daphnis.   Oh ! Ere too late !
To save her life I'd kill myself with haste.   [*Exeunt*

ACT V.

SCENE I.—*Temple of Artemis at Argos ; sacrificial altar.*

AGIS, MILO, EVADNE, IO *with the chaplets of a victim*, Priestess *discovered*, Soldiers, *&c.*

Agis. This is the crown, the sharp and central peak
Of our new realm, around whose base are piled,
Like lesser hills, palace and treasury,
And all that makes up Argos. But our grip,
Though firm, the dreadful Goddess will unclasp,
Yea smite us as king Idmon, save we yield
First to her will in this. Pyrrha, be hers !
And thou who sacrificial office dost,
Assure to us, even at such a price,
The kingdom !
Priestess. Kings do kingliest show who bow
Before the Gods, yet is your hope infirm.
The longest reign is shorter than a life,
A life at longest, short. On whom shall light
Threescore years hence your crown ?

Agis.   I do not know,
Only appease the Goddess !

    Priestess.   [*Breaking the salt-cakes on Io's head, and taking
        the knife*]   Artemis,
Giver of breath, take back the breath thou gav'st !
Our tribute of a life owns all life thine !

              Enter PYRRHA.

    Pyrrha.   Hold ! I am Pyrrha.

    Milo.   You are forward, girl.

    Pyrrha.   The maidens of the temple know my face,
Set me before them ! Let them then declare
Which Pyrrha, she or I.

    Priestess.   We have no eyes,
No ears, we yield the Goddess whom you will.
If a king's daughter what makes that to us ?
If it be not, what makes it ? We will show
In words the oracle, but not in deeds :
If you mistake, bear you the wrong !

    Agis [*to* Io].   Are you
Not Pyrrha, daughter to King Idmon ? Speak !
To claim it is to die.

    Pyrrha.   No, I am she !

    Io.   Who dares doubt who I am ? I stand prepared
To take what fate belongs to her I am.

    Milo.   This is but shuffling ; are you she or no ?

Io.   I am.

Pyrrha.   She is not.

Milo.   What perversity
Can make two maids, but to seem royally born,
Bid thus for death !

Pyrrha.   There was a woodman seized,
Who saw me fleeing ere I donned disguise—
Where is he?

Agis.   Bring this man before us.

Milo.   Sire,
That double traitor Creon, ere he fled,
Let the man go.

Pyrrha.   She has possessed herself
Of what I wore.   Let me be put to proof :
Let me the sanctuary's recesses thread
Where I was reared, and let her do the same.

Agis.   Let this proof be essayed.

Priestess.   Dread Lord, it may not.
If the Gods will that you should reign, their sign
Shall guide your choice, we will not aid.   We bend
Whate'er betide, to heaven, but the temple
We do forbid to all.

Milo [*to Agis*].   Let lots decide it.

Agis.   Chance is not fate : I will not trust to lots.
Presents will buy the truth.

Milo.   Or, maybe, lies.

The priestess Pyrrha shields, for her she reared ;
And loves her as her own.

Enter IDMON, *led by* DAPHNIS. AGIS *stands aghast, and*
EVADNE *marvels wherefore.*

[*To Evadne.*] It is King Idmon.
Agis.　　Hide thee in Hades !
I know that kings are mortal.
　　Evadne.　　　　　　　　He is flesh.
If it be Idmon, he escaped the bolt.
　　Idmon.　　Agis, not to let slip your realm as I,
I hear your purpose is, as mine was erst,
To slay my daughter.　Which though I had done,
In reparation I now yield my head
That had found shelter in the woods secure,
Even to what thou wilt, who art my foe,
In ransom of her life.
　　Agis.　　　　　　We have no will
To harm you.　But our throne no less demands
We sacrifice her.　Which of these is she,
If thou art Idmon, show us !
　　Idmon.　　　　　　I am blind,
Nor have, these ten years, seen her.
　　Evadne.　　　　　　　Pyrrha's voice
He knew.　Bid speak these maids.

Agis [*to Io*].   Speak, are you Pyrrha?

Io.   Albeit I must die that you may reign,
What I have said is said !

Agis [*to Idmon*].   Whose voice says this?

Pyrrha.   Io's !   O father, can she play my voice,
Until your ear tells not the counterfeit
From the true coin? You know that I am Pyrrha.

Io.   Father, you know my voice.   Am I not Pyrrha?

Agis.   Guide us, and yours are life and liberty.
Which voice is hers?

Idmon.   What do you think I am,
That I would not deceive you? Trust me not :
True to my daughter makes my words untrue :
If I say this is she and I say truth,
That truth betrays her to her death.

Milo [*to Daphnis*].   You, boy,
Do you know aught of these?

Daphnis   [*Aside*] One is my sister,
And one I love.   [*Aloud*] My Lord, how should I aught?

Agis.   Well then, one course remains.   That one is Pyrrha
We must believe ; for where could two be found,
As one of these must be, infatuate
To wrongly claim such danger?   To make sure
And found our empire as it were in rock,
Both shall be sacrificed !

Milo.   My liege, your cause
Long have I served in dark and doubtful deeds,

As well as fair ones. And I would not stick,
Since many bled to seat you where you sit,
At one's advised death. But in cold blood
To slay two maidens to make sure of one
Is wisdom pushed to ruthlessness.

    Agis.   Justly
She dies who dare such high estate usurp !

    Milo. I am not often touched. But let me plead
Once mercifully. You, Sire, have gotten offspring.
And just of such an age as these are now
Would be your first two children.

    Agis.   Tenderness
Is my steelèd bosom dead as they :
They both are gone.

    Milo.   Gone, but you know not dead.

    Agis. You said you saw them dead?

    Milo.   That was untrue.

    Evadne. [*Aside*] What will he say ?

    Milo. Listen, Evadne her own son to advance—
Crush me with vengeance, cruel I have been
But not a coward !—gave into my charge
Your girl and boy to slay them, telling you
That tale how robbers snatched them from your home.

    Agis. But you those robbers slew and brought their heads

    Milo. I slew two guiltless men and brought their heads,
And said your girl and boy I dead had found,
And laid them on the pyre. But in the woods

I left them living.   Not four summers old
The girl, the boy yet younger.   If they died
I know not.   But remember, while you strike,
Perhaps your children may that mercy need
That you deny.

  Agis. Milo, I trusted thee,
And thou hast paid my trust !   If this be true,
Let the seas roll between us ; but if false,
Thine is that death that else shall light on thee !
Evadne, dark Medea of our house !
Where are my children ?

  Daphnis [*aside*]. Left ? and in the woods ?
Sire, do not think me overbold, this chain
Do your eyes know ?

  Agis.   Yes ! round his neck my boy
That chain had ever clasped.   Where was it found ?

  Daphnis. 'Twas found on me ; and both found in the woods,
Sixteen years back.

  Agis. I think I see my bride
Look through your eyes.   My boy had on his neck
A ruddy mark.

  Daphnis. My liege, such mark have I. [*Bares his neck.*

  Agis. You are my son : your name is Hyacinth.
You, queen, expect your doom !   Where is my daughter ?

  Daphnis. Here, sire.

  Agis.   Ye Gods, in darkness toward what gulf
I trod !

But now my prisoned kindness, so long starved,
Would grace its freedom gained.   What would you, son,
That we, a king, may grant unto our son?

    Daphnis.   Sire, since my state is princely, and I stand
Her equal there, though in nought else, I crave,
With her consent, even this lady's hand.

    Agis.   If she be Pyrrha, worthy her estate!—
Though she be Pyrrha—mine be any fate,
She lives and shall be yours!

    Daphnis.   Fair maid, what answer?

    Pyrrha.   I am yours, Hyacinth.

    Priestess.   It is well said!
And now is riddled out the oracle
We gave but could not understand.   Behold
Life and not death delighteth Artemis,
Goddess of youth and noble womanhood.
Now let this wedding be the sacrifice
Even of life and self : self given up
To the World-Mother.

    Agis.   Here I yield my crown,
Fulfilling destiny, to your young head ;
Whose boyhood finds what we, too carefull, missed.
Rule henceforth, Hyacinth!

    Daphnis.   My first act
Makes Milo not an exile ; and revokes
Thy doom, defeated queen.   Rise free as air

For us !   But you, our father, in like mood
Take her back to thy breast.

    Agis.   I do forgive you.

    Daphnis.   Then sister mine, and more, my Pyrrha's friend,
We three part never.

    Priestess.   Thus your troubles end.
Happy young king, two kings, one proved and sage,
One skilled and brave, guard your scarce-ripened age.
Scorn not their counsel, yet your own deeds choose :
The Gods give—thine it is their gifts to use.

IN THE EVENING.

To-DAY our hearts are blithe though they remember sorrow.
Why should we borrow
 Out of the coming years
 Fewer hopes than fears ;
For to-day was once ' to-morrow ? '

Across the window draw the curtain.
 As a monarch metes his reign
Less by certain years than wars uncertain,
 So this eve we mete
 Less by the hours that beat
  As the old timepiece goes from chime to chime,
Than by drouth of cups we drain
 Or re-told memories, bitter-sweet,
  When heart and tongue grow freer with the time.

Pile the oak logs higher,
 Till the blue smoke dims the rafter.
  Evil fortune is not certain.
 Tell the tale with laughter,

As laugh the **oak logs stout**,
While we sit around the fire.
Across the window draw the curtain :
Care and Death stand close without.

LONDON : PRINTED BY
SPOTTISWOODE AND CO., NEW-STREET SQUARE
AND PARLIAMENT STREET

www.ingramcontent.com/pod-product-compliance
Lightning Source LLC
Chambersburg PA
CBHW020557270326
41927CB00006B/874